How To...
CHANGE it

HOW TO... CHANGE it

MAKE A DIFFERENCE

JOSHUA VIRASAMI

1 3 5 7 9 10 8 6 4 2

#Merky Books

20 Vauxhall Bridge Road

London SW1V 2SA

#Merky Books is part of the Penguin Random House group
of companies whose addresses can be found at global.
penguinrandomhouse.com.

Penguin
Random House
UK

First published in the United Kingdom by #Merky Books in 2020

www.penguin.co.uk

A CIP catalogue record for this book is available from the British Library.

ISBN 9781529118780

Text Design © Andreas Brooks

Typeset in 10/13 pt Source Serif Variable Roman by Jouve (UK), Milton Keynes

Printed and bound by Great Britain by Clays Ltd, Elcograf, S.p.A.

Penguin Random House is committed to a sustainable future for our
business, our readers and our planet. This book is made from
Forest Stewardship Council® certified paper.

MIX
Paper from
responsible sources
FSC® C018179

This book is dedicated to Shaun Mitchell, whose soul and fight lifted our spirits and showed us a better way of being with each other in the world.

Inna lillahi wa inna ilayhi raji'un.
Verily we belong to God, and verily
to Him do we return.
Qur'an, 2:156

CONTENTS

FOREWORD

I often think about these words: 'how to change it'. They are words that have long been reverberating inside my bones, with what feels like the ancestral challenge in my DNA, the call to action that so many of us have stepped up to. We, the community organisers, the youth who walked out of classrooms in protest, the ones collecting signatures and contact information outside of the jails that caged our loved ones, the involved parents and guardians of our children, and the neighbours that care too much – all of us who seemed so unassuming, but were taking notes. We took notes from the freedom fighters who were fighting side by side with us, and the ones we learned about from textbooks – but, as many of us will readily confess, we were making it up as we went along. No one could have prepared us for the challenges of twenty-first-century organising – not its global triumphs nor its insidious setbacks.

Growing up, I was not aware that organising was a thing that still existed. I grew up in the San Fernando Valley in California – a last vestige of the once suburban part of Los Angeles, which was now home to families like mine: poor, working-class, people of colour. I lived near the General Motors Assembly Plant in Van Nuys, an automobile factory that opened up in 1947. This automobile factory, as much as it was a health hazard for the community members who were forced to breathe in its pollution, was also the employer of the many black and brown men and women whose wages made it possible for their families to live with a decent quality of life. In fact, my father was a GM plant employee. His job was the reason my family had adequate health insurance. In the early 1980s, amidst the era of Reaganomics, the GM plant threatened to outsource, with little apparent remorse or afterthought of the devastation this would leave the families whose livelihood depended on it. Through the organising efforts of coalitions from all sectors, community organisers gathered church leaders, union workers, filmmakers, community members – everyone, essentially – to protest and boycott the closing of this plant. And it worked. The GM plant stayed open for another ten years.

This happened right in my neighbourhood, and yet I still had no idea how much organising had already impacted my life and the role it has played in changing entire systems. Much of my own organising work is rooted in the theories and philosophies of successful organisers around the world and throughout time. Whether it be Rigoberta Menchú, an indigenous freedom fighter from Guatemala, fighting for the rights of her people and indigenous people the world over. Or Angela Davis, a mentor and friend, who has laid the foundation for modern abolitionism within the United States and across the world. Each of these leaders lead not just with fierce passion, but also with a clear analysis of how we get to the goal: freedom.

Most of us do not grow up with a concept of organising or campaigning. When it is portrayed in the media, it's usually a one-dimensional display of the complex organism organising actually is. A caricature of a civil rights leader, say. We usually don't understand the role of strategy, and that organising is a science. With this writing project, Joshua is bringing a lifetime of personal and political experience to bear. When we are gifted books such as *How to Change It*, we are giving multiple generations an opportunity to show up for the resistance movement.

I am grateful to Joshua for outlining what resilience and change can look like for folks across the globe who are also thinking about these words, and, thankfully, here is a book that shows us how. How to change the material conditions for the most vulnerable. How to build power with the folks at the margins. And how to win when it feels like winning is absolutely impossible. When we are provided with tools to take on the very state that often interrupts our ability to live long and thriving lives, we are given an agency that only organising and campaign work can provide. Joshua is one of the most brilliant leaders of his time. I met him as he organised with Black Lives Matter UK. His values and principles are always at the centre of his organising; he was precise and clear while also being deeply compassionate. We need his voice to instruct us, to tell stories about us. We need his voice amplified to bring us together. Highlight the words that transform you. Underline and write out the definitions of new words that challenge you. Write on the page as though Joshua can hear you. Take these words as an opportunity to have a healing conversation. You need it. I need it. We all do.

This is how we show up. This is how we change it. This is how we take action.

Patrisse Cullors,
May 2020

INTRODUCTION

'We have to turn thinkers into fighters and fighters into thinkers'

General Gordan Baker, Jr, American labour organiser and activist

POLITICS HAPPENED TO ME

I wasn't at all political as a teenager. Youth politics was mostly for the more affluent kids at school. But politics happened *to* me, as it happened *to* most of my mates, and as it happens *to* most of us. I just didn't have any sense that I could do anything *to* politics in return. Things feeling unfair was a pretty constant theme for me as a young person, with shopkeepers banning me for theft I hadn't committed, librarians revoking me for noise I didn't make, police officers stopping and searching me for crimes I didn't commit, and head teachers suspending me for things I didn't participate in. I've never taken well to unnecessary interrogation. Why should I? To me, it seemed a lot of people I knew had a secret cop inside them, who wanted me to account for the most trivial things: 'Why do you have £200?', 'Why are you in this neighbourhood?' and so on.

For instance, one particular day at school, I was a bit rude to Mr Rogers, my secondary school Geography teacher. He'd asked me to leave the room before class had even started, after asking to see my behaviour report card. I'd replied, 'What does the previous lesson have to do with this one?', and so he sent me to the suspension room for the remainder of the day. Besides maybe a police cell, there were few rooms more boring than the one-person suspension room we had at school, and I'd spent the best part of many afternoons scratching tags into the desk and people-watching teachers using the printer nearby, but this time it felt like I was there for a week.

I had a complicated relationship with Mr Rogers, although he punished me a lot and for what felt like no good reason, he was also my gateway to beginning to see the world for what it is: broken. It was in his lessons that we looked at the links between child labour and high-street chains, where we understood climate change for the crisis it is, where wealth inequality and how the rich rule the world were cast at our feet, as the next generation, as *our* problem, as *political* problems. Through his lessons, a world of contradictions and divides became clear. A divide between the haves and the have-nots, between the global north and global south, between my world and everyone else's.

While Geography taught me there was a complicated world out there, my family's native country, Mauritius, *showed* it to me. Mauritius – a small East African island in the Indian Ocean – is a second home to me, and where most of my family live, including my mum now, and I used to go back to Mauritius almost yearly – until I had to pay the full adult fare. It's a place where worlds collide and merge, in its people and its culture; a country of Africans and Asians, of former slaves and former indentured labourers, of British and French colonialism. It's a country that pays the heavy cost of imposed underdevelopment, and will pay the future costs of the climate catastrophe. Realistically, it was all of these things that forced my family out, forced them right back here – to the supposed 'mother country': England, the very same country and colonial power that had once dragged their predecessors from India and Mozambique to Mauritius to begin with. As Sri Lankan writer and activist Ambalavaner Sivanandan once said, 'We are here, because you were there'.[1]

So, in Mr Rogers' class, when I wasn't being sent out for spurious reasons, I began to find a language that helped me describe a lot of what was going on in the world, but I was yet to find a voice with which to object to it all. That voice came much later on, when I withdrew from Loughborough University in 2010, went back to my borough of Hounslow and got a job pulling night shifts at the local Costa coffee, using the quiet moments to self-educate. I couldn't have foreseen the journey that lay ahead of me, but the language of protest came to me when I began to hear the voices of other people speaking back, and not just to a police officer or teacher, but speaking back to the whole damn system. When I heard the voice of Thomas Sankara[*] on YouTube, or the voice of Angela Davis,[†] then I knew where to begin to look for similar voices. Soon enough, I began to hear the voices of political movements all around the world and I realised that I, too, had a voice, that I have political agency, and that, collectively,

---

[*] Thomas Sankara was an anti-imperialist revolutionary and the first president of independent Burkina Faso, from 1983 to 1987.

[†] Angela Davis is an American political activist and author. She rose to international fame as a black revolutionary in 1970, when she was sent to prison for a crime she was later acquitted of, at a time when the US government was hell bent on putting activists of colour behind bars, using every trick in the book.

our agency is capable of transforming the world. But more than the iconic political movements I've had the honour of organising with, or the political giants I've had the pleasure of meeting, it's the towns, valleys, communities, cultures and projects that have transformed me into a firm believer in the inevitability of winning back the world, *if we fight*.

MAKE YOUR OWN MANUAL

There's no shortage of books and online materials illustrating the different ways to be an activist, but it's important to find your own groove, read widely and listen up. What you choose to do should always apply to your situation and to the wider context. Your activism needs to be locally rooted but international in vision. There will always be answers, but try to find questions. No matter what anyone tells you, *make your own manual*. I did.

I've learnt that winning is only inevitable if we recognise that our struggle is common, and it becomes common when we are all moved, collectively, by injustice. Although I reference my own life experiences in this book, the reason many of us often begin to protest and challenge inequalities is fundamentally about others as well as ourselves. We have a common sense of love in rage.[2] Regardless of our identity, our experiences and our context, we share this common internal resistance to injustice, which is born from the heart, and we therefore share a common struggle. This is the bedrock of solidarity, and solidarity is how we get free. Nearly all of us feel a deep discomfort at the direction the world has been heading, and a common desire for suffering and catastrophes to end. Although we hesitate to admit it, we know what is required to end this – the total transformation of many aspects of our lives, including our governing, economic and legal structures. What I hope this book adds to those sensations we share is the feeling and knowledge that this turning of the wheel requires the leadership, guidance and camaraderie of *every one of us*. Everyone has a contribution to make, big or small.

BUILD AND MOVE AS ONE

Not long after my first protest in London with Stop The War, in February 2011, I decided to become a member of a well-established socialist organisation, where I found myself in an entirely new world, connecting with hundreds of people, learning by doing. I spent the next few years moving around different types of political groups, protesting, organising, and, as a result sometimes getting entangled with the law. My family aren't from an inherently political background, and these movements and my new interest was all new to them. In the beginning, I remember my mum stressing out; she was worried I had joined a cult when I kept travelling into central London for strategy meetings. However, for all the power and the determined people I came across in those first few years, I found nearly none of *my* people, the people who raised me, the people I'd grown up with, and that was a problem. Like most people in those meetings, I travelled far away from home to *do* politics. With time, I've realised that this is not how we build power. The fact is, if we want real power, people power, we need to be *with* our communities and workplaces in the struggle, strategising how we get strong and get free collectively as one. Many people whose names we campaign in, whose experiences we draw righteous anger from, are oftentimes reluctant to join political activism. It's no surprise, though. In Britain, so much self-described political activism happens away from the day-to-day conversations in communities, and away from many people's lived experiences. If our work colleagues, our local schools, our neighbours, our congregations, our people are absent, we're wasting the genius, creativity, experience, wisdom and power that are the ingredients needed to transform the world.

My community is working class. The vast majority of my mates and I either worked in the hospitality industry, as servers or waiters, done admin-related office jobs, warehouse roles in retail. Most of our parents were cleaners, care workers, dinner ladies, nurses, receptionists, local teachers, shopworkers or had small businesses. My mum did part-time care work, while my dad ran a one-person shipping company and was also a taxi driver on the side. These are the real arenas of political struggle, this is where we need to be politically organised. This is where our power is. On the shop floors, in warehouses, care homes, schools, housing blocks, office buildings, taxi ranks and also with those jobs without a physical workplace, seeing as a growing minority of the world works in the informal economy, such as delivery cyclists, private-hire drivers or virtual assistants. There are also the areas of work that go unrecognised as 'work', because they are often unwaged, such as domestic work and child-raising – the work of producing life. These spheres are where the power needed to change the world lies, as it is *us* who make the economy, society, *everything* possible. The people made to work the most insecure jobs, on the lowest pay, with the least access to decent healthcare and other public services – these people are the backbone of this country, particularly those who are racialised or are migrants.

> **NOTE:** I often use the word 'racialised' in this book to describe people, be they Roma, Jewish or Black etc. Race isn't permanent or static: it is an unnatural and enforced social process, and has been for several hundred years; no one is born with a race, they are *racialised*.

YOU AND ME

I think the moment I first began to realise we needed to take action and escalate was back in school, all those years ago in a stuffy classroom next to the library. Mr Rogers stood in front of us and explained to the class about what climate change was and is. It drew me in, and he continued using two words that I didn't understand at first, but, when I did, I could never forget: magnitude and frequency. In the coming years, the *magnitude* and *frequency* of natural disasters would increase dramatically, he told us. Heatwaves, wildfires, droughts, hurricanes, flooding. Natural disasters have very real consequences. At current rates of global warming, by 2050 it's estimated there'll be over 200 million climate refugees, and every single one of these refugees is a person, like you and me, all forced to leave their homes, their lives, their families. By 2070, it's estimated that one third of all plant and animal species could be extinct. That day I remember going home and telling my family about that lesson, and that was the only time in my school career I'd ever shared what I learnt in school. Climate change is *not* accidental, just as economic crises, war, unemployment and poverty aren't either: they are deeply, deeply political, and they require political action to remedy them, and this political action requires you and me.

The world is in unparalleled upheaval, the likes of which we've not seen since the second World War. If you're my age – twenty-nine – you will have lived through a wave of world-changing events: 9/11, the Iraq War, the 2008 Global Financial Crisis, Austerity Britain, the 2011 England Riots, the Arab Spring, the global Coronavirus pandemic and the rise of far-right nationalism in some of the world's most powerful countries, with leaders such as Narendra Modi in India, Donald Trump in the USA, Benjamin Netanyahu in Israel, Viktor Orbán in Hungary, Jair Bolsonaro of Brazil, and, right here in the UK, Boris Johnson, just to name some of the most obvious. We're at a crucial moment, which calls for fighting back – and by that I mean getting together, getting educated, getting organised and getting our hands on power.

It's possible, however, as we look forward, to also look back and see useful parallels in history, some of it quite recent. For example, the Zapatistas' revolutionary seizure of Chiapas, Mexico, in 1994,*

---

* The EZLN (Zapatista Army of National Liberation), is a revolutionary organisation made up of mostly rural and indigenous people. In 1994 they occupied seven towns throughout the eastern half of Chiapas, in Southern Mexico,

the Rojava revolution of 2011 in Northern Syria,[*] and the Sudanese uprising of 2018–19.[†] Then there are the thousands of community campaigns, large and small, here and in other countries, throughout history that have championed the downtrodden and won, whether that's bringing about the scrapping of the sexist Page Three from the *Sun* newspaper or abolishing unjust Section-21 'no-fault' evictions. When we fight back against

---

and began to establish a network of cooperatives, healthcare and education systems as well as radical autonomous political, economic and cultural structures.

[*] Rojava, otherwise known as the Democratic Federation of Northern Syria, is a region where over 4 million people live, and where a revolutionary experiment is taking place. Through a self-developed political system, known as Democratic Confederalism, the principles of ecology, feminism and direct democracy have reshaped society, governance and relationship to the land. The book *Revolution in Rojava: Democratic Autonomy and Women's Liberation in Syrian Kurdistan* by Michael Knapp, Ercan Aybboga, and Aja Flach (London: Pluto Press, 2016) is a good starting point if you want to understand the dynamics, history and lessons we can learn from Rojava.

[†] From late 2018 to 2019, following years of economic mismanagement, austerity, corruption and human rights abuses, hundreds of protests and sustained strikes toppled the rule of then President; Omar al-Bashir

injustice and win on a local level, I would argue, we create a ripe environment for people to feel empowered to fight bigger battles. When we fight back bigger, on a national level, we create a ripe environment for movements around the world to then feel empowered to fight back where they are, globally, such as with the #BlackLivesMatter movement. When we connect our fights across boroughs, across national borders – as we should, because we face common enemies – when we build an international platform for systemic change, we create a ripe environment for revolution.

WE NEED A VISION

I've spent ten years completely engrossed in the question of 'what is to be done?' A question that has taken me everywhere from BBC newsrooms to community centres and even to the Old Bailey. Along the way, I've been criticised by tabloids and I've been smeared by people I've organised alongside. But despite all that, and most importantly, I've never stopped learning, and I've never stopped taking notes. Whether sat in negotiations with the City of London as a representative of the Occupy movement, sat across the table from renowned

American political activist, philosopher and academic Angela Davis, or sat in an occupied London estate scheduled for demolition alongside many fellow everyday heroes, I've picked up on some of what it takes to build mass movements capable of lifting us all out of the miserable conditions we find ourselves in. Above all, I've learned the most through my mistakes, and I implore you as you read this book to not give up and to try and try again, because this is messy work, riddled with the gift of failure, and that is just its nature.

In working to make change, at whatever level, we need to think about what comes next, which means putting our imagination to work, thinking about how people can live, love, work and prosper. We need a vision. What does twenty-first-century Socialism for the many look like? What does transformation in how we relate to each other look like? And then we need answers. Frantz Fanon,* writing about

---

* Frantz Fanon was a psychiatrist, revolutionary fighter and political philosopher born in the French colony of Martinique who went on to become one of the most important writers during the anti-colonial liberation struggle. Fanon participated in the Algerian war of independence and his works on the impact of colonisation and racism have influenced liberation movements across the world and through time.

his experiences of racism and war, offered us a vision of a revolutionary humanism: a politics that says that, no matter what divides us, we're all connected by our common humanity. It's not always easy to conjure this vision, as many of us live lives that are cash, space and time poor. But, amid the governmental neglect, the insurgent far-right nationalisms, the climate catastrophe and so much more, there can be found the taste of freedom: the better nature that we appeal to, of social solidarity, which always emerges in moments of crisis. Just look around us now in 2020, as I write – even in a global pandemic, we're seeing millions begin to embrace mutual aid across communities and cities.

WHAT THIS BOOK IS AND ISN'T

But, before anything else, I'd like to potentially save you some time by saying what this book is and isn't. This book is not a 'top ten tips on how to protest', it's also not a 'how-to-fuck-shit-up manual'. However, if you're here because of Grenfell, Bojo, Brexit, Coronavirus or any other very political catastrophe that has awoken a rage within you, you're in the right place. If you're here because you're sick of law enforcement, your landlord, your boss or the endless bills and debt thrown at you/society, then you're still in the right place. If you're here because you're interested in people power, and how we actualise it, then you are *definitely* in the right place.

Though, as much as this book offers suggestions, I hope it prompts questions too. Last year, during a community project I was facilitating, we were filming an exercise where the group commented on each other's experience as local renters and one of the participants said the following, which stuck with me:

> 'Who's benefiting from the fact that, in order to get decent housing at a decent standard [. . .] you need to be broken. Who's benefiting from the people in this room being broken?
>
> There must be someone, somewhere at the end of all of this, that wants most of society, most of the working class, to be broken.
>
> That's the thing we need to think about getting across, that's a question we want to put to our audience: at the end of the day, who are the people who are engineering this?'

One of the points of this book is to push us all to keep asking the right questions, of ourselves, our communities and those supposedly in charge. Whatever level of change we're seeking to create, we need to know how to ask the right questions, to interrogate and seek the truth.

EDUCATE, ORGANISE, AGITATE

How to Change It is structured into three key parts, or lessons: educate, organise, agitate. Those three words are derived from a slogan that has been a basis for many schools of political activism for over a century. Popularised by one of the leaders of Indian independence, B. R. Ambedkar, 'educate, agitate, organise' has been a methodology for political activism for countless left-wing movements. The phrase originated with a radical pamphlet written by social activist and leader of the Arts and Crafts Movement William Morris, for the first Socialist party in England, the Democratic Federation of Socialists, in which he urged all of us to engage with the fight for justice and freedom. Wisdom is an activist's best friend, and 'educate, organise, agitate' is a collective wisdom, drawn from centuries of struggle, knowledge, experience and insight.

The slogan has had different meanings at different points in history, but, in this instance:

EDUCATE: is about reclaiming our minds. We look at how we revolutionise the mind, name what the system is, how it works, and how history can illuminate not just the present, but the path ahead of us. Once you are able to name your enemies, and explain their illogic, then you need to know how to get organised.

ORGANISE: is about reclaiming our fight. We explore what it means to organise ourselves, to create strategy and to make strong groups that are accessible and can navigate organising in today's hypersurveilled world. With an understanding of the terrain, a group to organise with and a plan, we then need to take action, and win.

AGITATE: is about reclaiming our power. We see what agitation, or direct action, is and how we can do it, exploring the importance of civil disobedience and political education as possible tactics for building power and creating crises for our opponents.

WE CAN WIN

Of course, it could be argued that we don't need anything written in this book to be able to go out there and make a change in the world. With courage in our hearts, we may create real power guided only by intuition. However, history suggests that fortune favours the brave and the prepared far more. Therefore, I hope that, as transformation is a double-edged sword I hope within this book, you will find opportunities to tackle not just the enemies around you, but also the enemies within. I hope, too, that you find answers and inspiration, as much as you find confidence and purpose. The world needs *you* for change to be possible, so get educating, agitating and organising. *We can win*.

EDUCATE

PLAYLIST

This playlist is selected to invoke remembering, reclaiming and renewal as education. Whether it's Little Simz's reclamation over her wings, Burna Boy remembering Britain's role in plundering Nigeria or Kano's prayer for new beginnings.

Black The Ripper ft. Dot Rotten – 'This Is for'
Queen Latifah – 'U.N.I.T.Y.'
Little Simz – 'Wings'
Sudan Archives – 'Nont For Sale'
Potter Payper – 'Carpe Diem'
Oscar #Worldpeace – 'Invent'
Billie Holiday – 'Strange Fruit'
Maverick Sabre – 'Guns in the Distance'
Burna Boy ft. M.anifest – 'Another Story'
Lauryn Hill – 'Final Hour'
Nipsey Hussle ft. CeeLo Green – 'Loaded Bases'
Bob Marley and The Wailers – '400 years'
Kano – 'A Roadman's Hymn'
Sly and The Family Stone – 'Everyday People'

Education in Britain has long been an arena of political struggle. As black feminist activists Beverley Bryan, Stella Dadzie and Suzanne Scafe wrote back in 1985, in *Heart of the Race: Black Women's Lives in Britain,* 'the education system's success can be measured directly in terms of black children's failure within it'.[1] Nothing has changed; as the National Education Union was still pointing out in 2018, 'differences in the social background of pupils are the primary factors causing inequality in educational outcomes.'[2] One third of all UK pupils are poor and working class, and a disproportionate amount of this group are ethnic minorities. This divide has created a two-tiered education system.

The experience of education in Britain is extremely polarised. On one hand, you have schools in disproportionately poor, racialised and under-privileged areas that have been arguably increasingly profitised, and which often feed the school-to-prison pipelines that reliably start with the injustice of school exclusions for racialised youth. On the other, you have two-hundred-year-old or more private schools serving as a school-to-power pipeline, preparing a certain class of people – the ruling class – for leadership roles within the government, mainstream media, corporate boardrooms or the military.

In this environment, the majority of us – the non-elite – are simply herded through education and prepared for work, with our thinking standardised, normalised, and, as American philosopher and linguistics expert Noam Chomksy writes, 'geared to obedience'.[3] We leave education and face a reality of under-employment, squalid private renting and constant economic crises, and we generally don't leave compulsory education knowing how to make sense of these experiences. We don't learn how to both read and navigate a very political world. Most importantly, we don't learn how the world got into this state in the first place.

It is in this context of mass indoctrination that we approach 'Educate'. Becoming revolutionary starts with the mind, with overcoming our miseducation. It's a constant process, but we need to revolutionise our thinking by finding language and beginning to name our enemies, and bring them out into the open. We need to look at the mechanics of indoctrination, seek out ideology and debunk it. Most importantly, we need to return to the people's history, and be reminded of the revolutionary minds that have defined the course of it over the last centuries. By taking these steps, we can loosen the grip of the system on our mind, learn to re-humanise one another, and be better prepared to organise for power, and for freedom.

CHAPTER 1

KNOW YOURSELF

FINDING THE LANGUAGE

Around the age of eight, I used to get into a lot of fights at school. One day, I got in an argument with another boy in my class. It began to escalate, and the boy suddenly said something upsetting about my skin colour. That was my first conscious experience of racism, and it struck me down. I vividly remember my mum coming into school to discuss it with the teachers. In that moment I was branded by race, and violated for something I could never change. It opened a wound, one that has never healed.

Fast forward a few years: I was fifteen, and I had got my first job, as a dishwasher at a busy weekend carvery. Coincidentally, it was near where my mum was first employed when she arrived in the UK in 1989, where she worked challenging shifts in a care home. I worked hard, and was paid £3.77 an hour. One day, a colleague let it slip that my hard work helped produce the profits that paid our company CEO £585,000 a year.

Both these experiences felt completely unnatural, and unjust, yet they were as normal to everyday life as going to school or washing the dishes. It took a lot more experiences similar to those above to help me understand the inequity of the world we live in, but they were the starting points in many ways. They began to give me the language I needed to name and attempt to overcome injustice, and know myself better.

No one ever gave me the vocabulary to explain why me and my family would be stared at if we visited the English countryside, or why I would be repeatedly stopped and searched by police, and why my peers had to submit labour below minimum wage.

I had spent fifteen years in school, yet there was an utter absence of any language or concepts with which to explain my own and my family's everyday experiences of class and racism. More than that, with every teacher who assumed I was stupid, with every underpaid monthly wage, and, as I got older, every job-seeker's interview that turned into a cross-examination, I began to believe that both the small and the large everyday injustices were just facts of life, and there was nothing I could do. When I finally found the language to name the systems, such as 'racial capitalism', I gained a sense of vindication; I realised how much bullshit I had blindly accepted, how much adjusting I had done to fit in with the way things were, especially when the way they were was unjust. Without this vocabulary, every instance had seemed like a personal attack. Although music and culture had showed me that the system existed, it was only through hearing the voice of Malcolm X[*] in my head, attacking a global system of white supremacy, or the voice of trade unionist Tom Mann[†] attacking a global system of class exploitation, that I could finally see a context within which my experiences sat. Now, prepared with the vocabulary, I could begin to understand it and call it as I felt it.

Some years later, as an organiser with Black Lives Matter UK, I met Albert Woodfox and Robert King, two members of the Angola Three – three prisoners turned Black Panthers,[‡] who collectively served over

---

[*] Malcolm X was a prominent and controversial civil rights leader in the US. Many of his theories became the blueprint for Black Power movements in the 1960s and 1970s. He was assassinated when he was thirty-nine.

[†] Tom Mann was a labour leader, and member of numerous British labour unions and organisations between the 1880s and 1930s, and famously fought tooth and nail for an eight-hour work day.

[‡] The Black Panther Party was a black revolutionary socialist political organisation who coordinated within working class black communities in the 60s–80s, building a mass movement.

one hundred years in twenty-three-hour lockdown in the Louisiana State Penitentiary, otherwise known as 'Angola', the largest maximum security prison in America. The three men met in prison, but had near-identical histories, and had been repeatedly arrested for breaking Jim Crow laws. They had all discovered the revolutionary socialist politics of the Black Panther Party, an insurgent ideology they then developed, held on to and helped spread while incarcerated in Angola. Over tea and digestive biscuits that day, Woodfox and King recounted some painful memories of their time in prison, such as the occasions when they were beaten within an inch of their lives for encouraging other prisoners to question their circumstances and conditions. Together, these prisoners had begun to *name* the injustices they were facing, and set up a chapter of the Black Panther Party within the prison, where they taught fellow inmates maths, grammar and revolutionary theory. Robert King explained to us how everything changed when he

---

The Panthers fought for and established real economic, social, and political equality through mass organising and community programs. Check out their Ten-Point Program online: http://blackpower.web.unc.edu/2017/04/the-black-panthers-10-point-program/

finally found the words to describe the injustice he had lived with his whole life. In the work of the Black Panther Party, he found a voice, one that helped him situate his story – his journey through the criminal justice system, his experience as a working-class black man, and his seemingly random and personal misfortunes – within a wider context. It was at this point that Robert King became an agent of change in his own life, irrespective of whether he was incarcerated, because he was finding the language to explain and critique the wrongs done to him. To really know ourselves, we need to constantly be seeking a language to name injustice and exploitation.

THE MATRIX

It's a bit like what Morpheus describes to Neo in the iconic 'blue pill, red pill' scene in *The Matrix*:*

---

* Tragically, 'the red pill' and 'red pilling' is also a phrase being claimed by violently misogynistic 'incels', young men who come together in often 'alt-right' online communities, to mean being 'awoken' to the reality of how society has been 'brainwashed' by feminists, Marxists, anti-racists and liberals. Bharath Ganesh's 2018 *Fair Observer* article, 'What the Red Pill Means For Radicals', does a great job at debunking some of those arguments.

'What you know you can't explain, but you feel it. You've felt it your entire life, that there's something wrong with the world.' Of course, we are not literally living in the Matrix, but there *is* something deeply wrong with our world. Perhaps the most important line comes a few scenes later, when Morpheus answers the all-important question from Neo: 'What is the Matrix?', and Morpheus replies, 'Control'. Control is an important concept in helping us articulate how the systems that control us in real life work. The key question to ask, then, is control over what? In the movie, Morpheus answers this too, saying that the Matrix is 'a prison for your mind'. If revolutionising our thinking is about transforming our mind, then preserving it as it is, controlling it, is the opposite. However, as the Angola Three understood intimately, we are often imprisoned both psychologically and physically – not only in prisons but in our workplaces, schools, and even our family homes. Prisons, low-paid labour and unpaid labour are all means of caging humans physically, but this physical confinement is intertwined with psychic confinement. For the ruling class, both bodies and minds need to be controlled and contained, but it's never a complete project: caged birds still dream of faraway places, and sometimes they get there.

The idea of the prison of the mind is not new. Legendary singer and songwriter Bob Marley told us, in his aptly titled 'Redemption Song', to liberate ourselves mentally and physically from enslavement. Marley was referencing the need to escape 'Babylon' – a term commonly used by Black people to describe the exact site of their oppression from the days of slavery to now. 'Babylon' and 'the matrix' are terms I grew up with; they were used interchangeably by my mates to describe what others might call 'the system' or 'capitalism', or what academic-activist bell hooks calls the 'imperialist, capitalist, white-supremacist patriarchy'.[4] This might be a mouthful, but it's a useful phrase, as you need to be able to name your enemy.

The ultimate success of control is to create unquestioning people in an unquestioning environment. We live in a world where powerful nations and corporations pursue completely irrational and destructive aims, destroying people and the planet through war, environmental degradation, and the ruthless pursuit of profit. Morpheus tells Neo there's only one way out and that is to: 'free your mind'. In reality, there is only one way we can all free our minds: by asking questions, revolutionising our thinking and believing that another way is possible.

ANSWERING BACK

Growing up, teachers said I couldn't 'control my mouth', and while I admit I might have had a bit of a bad attitude, I always felt that 'questioning back' didn't really warrant the level of punishment they gave me. However, their reaction to my constant questions is symbolic of our wider punitive culture against people who ask uncomfortable questions and challenge authority. I was inquisitive as a child, and I loved to read. When I was five or six, my family moved out of our tower block and into a small bungalow opposite the local library. I pursued my love for books and made good use of the children's section, finding new answers to the many questions I had back then. But it wasn't until I was older that I began to lose my childlike inquisitiveness and grapple with some very uncomfortable questions. Recently, my dad showed me the letter I wrote explaining why I had decided to take myself out of university. In the letter, I said that 'I had become weighed down by heavy questions surrounding the gross injustices plaguing the world.' I told them I had to quit university and 'apply myself to figuring out how I could best make a difference'. Feeling the need to pause and try to fix things in the world is a fundamental truth in all of us I suspect, but not all of us feel empowered to follow our instincts.

The great Greek philosopher Socrates once said that we cannot assume that those in power are guided by truth and rigour. Therefore, it's on us to develop 'critical analysis', and to do so by questioning the world, and taking time to revolutionise our minds. This means examining the gross inequalities and injustices that characterise our environment, questioning the justifications offered by the powerful, and seeking out our own evidence and alternatives. This is not just limited to criticising the powerful, but also involves reflecting on our own thoughts and actions. At best, our restless questioning of everything should serve as a path to humility and personal growth. The anti-apartheid revolutionary Steve Biko* said something that I

---

* Steve Biko was a South African anti-apartheid activist, co-founder of the South African Student's Organisation and leader of the Black Consciousness Movement in the late 1960s

hold close: 'the most potent weapon in the hands of the oppressor, is the mind of the oppressed.'[5] To turn this on its head, a revolutionary mind might just be the most *potent* weapon in the *hands of the oppressed*.

Being able to name our enemies, to critically question injustice, is the most dangerous skill in the eyes of those who control nation states and multinational corporations: they prefer unthinking workers and uncritical consumers. In the eyes of the powerful, the perfect worker, the perfect machine, is one that leads an unexamined life. But Socrates and many others have told us that an unexamined life was not worth leading. And so, when we examine our condition closely, and reflect on our experiences of limited freedom, exploitation and oppression, there is only one conclusion that presents itself: we cannot become adjusted to the thinking of the times, instead we must revolutionise our thinking, to know ourselves and know the world.

---

and 70s. Biko was forbidden from writing or public speaking in '73, in '77 he died from injuries sustained whilst in police detention.

CHAPTER 2

KNOW THE WORLD

X MARKS THE SPOT

It was a hot spring day in Lahore, Pakistan. I had journeyed there cross-country over three weeks, on my way to the Wagah border into India. I'd spent that afternoon with a friend, roaming the campus of Lahore's National College of Arts, where his sister was a teacher. We'd had a great conversation, and before I left she dropped a copy of *The Autobiography of Malcolm X* into my hand. 'Keep it,' she said. That night, hiding from the mosquitoes beneath the bedsheet, I flicked on my little torch and started reading. From bed-to-bus-to-train, Malcolm X's words provided more than an awakening: they were instructive, they were infectious. They told me to get educated, and know myself. But he also made me dig further, and question what we know of the world around us. Revolutionary thinking requires that you not just name the system, but that you suss it out too. What makes it work? Who does it serve? *Knowing* the world is never a complete process, but *starting* to explain it is what is important, pulling back the curtains and peering into some of the inner mechanics. By doing so, we notice that, far from an innocent structure, the system works hard to manufacture consent and discourage dissent, and, importantly, we notice where it can be interrupted and unveiled for the sham that it is.

UNDERSTANDING IDEOLOGIES

> **DEFINITION: IDEOLOGY** – a set of beliefs, ideas, symbols, meanings and histories that work to legitimise a dominant political power, Marx extended this to assert that it is through ideological dominance that the ruling class legitimise and enable their oppression and exploitation.

Ideology is one of the single most important terms I've learned. Ideologies provide the logic for the ruling class' grip on power. In a capitalist society, these ideologies are reproduced in the criminal justice system, the education system, the mass media, science, religion and the family.

I grew up consuming a lot of television, everything from local news, *MTV*, *Eastenders*, *Blue Peter*, *The Simpsons*, *Buffy*, *Dragonball Z* to *Channel U*. I also enjoyed listening to the radio and my collection of CDs, be it Eminem, Destiny's Child or Skepta mixtapes, and as a family, we went to church. These moments were all an education in and of themselves. Through music videos, storylines, representations and sermons, I began to develop a lens with which to understand gender roles, what to expect in the world of work, how romantic and sexual relationships work and more. All of my consumption imparted a certain kind of unquestioned, uncritical 'common sense' to my adolescent mind: on the virtues of the rich and the vices of the poor, the natural relationship of boss and worker, the kind of work I was fit for, what it meant to be British, and, importantly, who remains excluded from Britain. The latter came in the form of questioning and suspicion – broadcasted on the news, or heard in person – an idea of who really belongs, what clothing doesn't fit with Britain's respectable self-image, and what race those people have to be.

All these ideas, beliefs and values together are representative of the dominant ideologies of Western society, but, in brief, they are:

IMPERIALIST – because of the belief in the superiority and entitlement of Western civilisation to the resources of the Global South.

CAPITALIST – because of the belief in the superiority of the ruling class over the worker.

WHITE SUPREMACIST – because of the belief in the superiority of whites over racialised people.

PATRIARCHAL – because of the belief in the superiority of the cis-straight male over those who identify as women and/or as queer.

NOTE: Whatever your journey, you will probably hear of Karl Marx. Marx saw capitalism as an exploitative economic system that divided people into classes based on their role in the economy: the ruling classes, who own the 'means of production' and set wages and prices in order to make a profit and amass more capital; and the workers, who are forced to sell their labour to the ruling classes for a wage in order to survive. The focus on profit, which characterises capitalist society, means that 'relations of production' are exploitative and oppressive, creating dangerous, low paid and unpaid working environments.

One class of people benefits from and reproduces the dominance of these ideologies, and one class only – the ruling class: the heads of industries, heads of government, heads of militaries, and heads of media. Together these ideologies legitimise the expropriation of resources from the global south, and the oppression and the exploitation of the working class, most notably women and minorities. This elite global group operates through a revolving door, often switching roles from one position of control and power to the other. Take, for example, George Osborne, who went from implementing a policy of austerity throughout Britain as its Chancellor of the Exchequer one day to being editor of London newspaper the *Evening Standard* the next. When one social group, such as the ruling class, uses social systems to spread ideologies, whether through education, mass media or policing and the court systems, they cement and justify their dominance through fixing the norms and values of societal culture.

This process is what Antonio Gramsci[*] called 'hegemony'.

---

[*] Antonio Gramsci was an Italian Marxist philosopher and communist politician. He was imprisoned under Mussolini's fascist regime and published most of his writing from prison.

> **DEFINITION: HEGEMONY** – the leadership, or dominance/power, by one state or social group over others. This concept helps us understand how dominant ideologies spread and become part of our social norms, morals and values, and how we learn to respond to their symbols. These symbols can be anything from how we dress to our skin colour.

In Britain, there is a dominant ethno-nationalist ideology. It's the same ideology that drove my mum's work colleague to tell her to 'go back to where she came from', even after twenty-eight years of her living here. It is one of the underpinning ideologies that made my mother's homeland a British slave colony – underdeveloped and exploited for the enrichment of the country she was compelled to migrate to for a better life. The dominant patriarchal ideology is why many of my friends have experienced domestic abuse, sexual violence or transphobia. None of this is natural, none of this should be normal, all of this is the ideological violence of hegemony.

One example of how this hegemony works is in justifying the war on terror, Islamophobia and the heightened state surveillance of Muslim communities around the world. One afternoon I was walking through a busy Leicester Square and moved aside for an older gentleman to pass, saying, 'Here you go, brother'. He stopped, squared up to me, and shouted: 'I'm not your brother, you head-chopping Muslim bastard!' A crowd formed around us, and I politely asked if we could step aside and talk. He obliged, and we ended up talking for nearly an hour. Our interaction was tense at first, but soon enough we were laughing, swapping stories and ultimately learning from each other. I shared my own life experiences to suggest that we may have had more in common than meets the eye. Most downtrodden people can generalise from their own experiences of oppression and exploitation to connect with and be in solidarity with other people's experiences I find, even though they may be different. He pushed back, but slowly began to appreciate my position and open up. He confessed that, as he grew older and his circles grew smaller, he wound up with a regular group of friends at the pub, who all followed tabloid news, which in turn built up his prejudices. In his words, his distancing from me, 'his neighbour', began with the reporting of the mass media.

MASS MEDIA AND ITS INFLUENCE

Mass media and especially news corporations have played a fundamental role in forming our consciousness of the idea of the superiority of Western mores, culture and society over Islamic mores, culture and society. For the passerby I connected with, his viewpoint wasn't controversial: it was commonsense. Therefore, we must be aware of how hegemony can be disseminated through mass media, but, as he also pointed out, it continues in our social groups and friendship networks, and this is how it becomes firmly rooted in culture. His experience is not unique; we all have hegemonised minds we must work on, social groups that reproduce harmful hegemony, and beliefs that help us remain divided and unable to find common cause in battling the socio-economic domination of those ruling over us. The older gentleman from Leicester Square didn't have a mobile phone, so I left him my email address. I never heard from him, but I hope he remembers our exchange as fondly as I do.

COMMON SENSE IS NOT SO COMMON

My dad has a saying he's fond of repeating: 'Common sense is not so common.' Basically, it shouldn't be trusted that it's a given. We often see claims for 'common sense' touted when people see themselves as guardians of the national interest, when people suddenly feel obliged to protect law and order, to protect borders or to protect the economy: at that moment, people, who can otherwise have a good sense of camaraderie with their neighbour, begin to wheel out ideology as a supposedly common-sense approach.

EXERCISE: Think of relevant news stories that demonstrate hegemony and ideology. Maybe you've heard some of the following: Migrants 'abuse the benefits system' and black communities are 'a hotbed of criminal activity'. If so, where might you have heard them? Because of the frequent distortion of truth, we are led to believe we should police and criminalise both these communities.

I've been an organiser with Black Lives Matter UK since 2016, helping to organise demonstrations, community meetings, talks, events, and our organisational strategy. We are connected to the US cohort and, like them, our overall aim is to build a political movement towards Black liberation. In 2016, on the anniversary of the death of Mark Duggan, the twenty-nine-year-old black man shot dead by police in Tottenham, North London, whose death sparked riots, Black Lives Matter UK took direct action in London, Nottingham, Manchester and Birmingham by shutting down highways. We were taking a stand against the abhorrent racism inherent in immigration, education and policing in this country, and we were invited on to dozens of TV and radio shows. In one instance, one of our members ended up in a strange debate with a caller to a radio programme, who shared that he grew up around black people, and how he thought everyone knew that drugs and criminality are a part of the black community. This sentiment and misconception is commonly held, sadly. Perhaps Britain's most influential TV host, Piers Morgan, for example, has a tendency to talk about youth violence in the capital as a distinctly 'black-on-black issue'. To many people it has become 'common sense' that youth violence is endemic to working-class black and brown communities, including even those of us from those very communities.

But serious youth violence is an issue of class inequality primarily, not race, exacerbated by a decade of brutal austerity and over policing in working-class communities. In Glasgow, which experienced a similar crisis, coincidentally, it was void of racist mythologies clouding the issue, as most of the young people were white, thus the local government responded, taking a public health approach. While they amplified policing in Glasgow – increasing the stop and searches many black and brown youths are all too familiar with – they also did something else too, something that proved transformative. Unlike most English cities, which have seen severe cuts to youth services, Glasgow put more investment into youth clubs, addiction services and mental health specifically for young people. They also stopped school exclusions, which is another key to why young people are often mislabelled unfairly as outcasts, making their lives an uphill struggle before they've even reached adulthood. It is this myth making, the consequences of sustaining ruling-class hegemony, that we can't afford to ignore and which we have to interrogate when we examine our lives and suss out the system.

TIP

Although I've talked about how culture can impart ideology, it can also, conversely, provide cutting critiques of dominant ideologies. When we look for ways to suss out the system, we will often find it in the studies of people like Italian-American academic and activist Silvia Federici and Jamaican born British sociologist and cultural theorist Stuart Hall, but we can also find it in the novels of Gabriel Garcia Marquez or Octavia Butler. We'll find it in the cinema of Gurinder Chadha or Ken Loach, just as we might find it in the lyrics of Kano and Princess Nokia.

HOOD INTELLECT

My school work experience was at an airport, and, if I'm honest, was less work experience and more a break from the monotony of school. After all, by the age of thirteen, I'd already worked as a paperboy, and had done odd jobs in the warehouse with my dad. I'd got myself a placement at the airport concierge service. The early morning public bus from Hounslow to Heathrow airport was full of people from the local community – as one of the places with always available jobs, it was a magnet for most. My bus was full of tired, underpaid black and brown faces like mine. I'd catch the 111 bus late in its journey and secure a spot on the top deck, the inside seat right by the window. It's the same bus I'd catch to go chill at my mate's house, or to go get curly fries from Rocky's kebab shop on the high road. I used to play one album I was borrowing from a mate on repeat up and down those journeys: *Welcome to Jamrock* by reggae singer Damian Marley. I'd listen to 'Confrontation', 'Road to Zion' and 'Khaki Suit' back to back. I'd rap to myself while making cups of tea at work. It was a point of conversation with my boss, who bought me Dr Dre's album *Chronic* and Ice Cube's *Lethal Injection* as parting gifts. Music to me then, as it is now, became another language to contextualise the injustices I knew or saw, here and in Mauritius.

Alongside the poetry and prose we were made to study at school, most of my friends and I learnt the lyrics of the musicians we listened to. In the early noughties it was Jehst, Styles P, Shystie, Klashnekoff, Ms Dynamite, Nas, Lauryn Hill, 2Pac, Roll Deep, Sizzla, So Solid, Kano, Ghetts, P Money,

Big Narstie, and the list goes on. Through the extra-curricular education they gave us, we came to a number of clear positions, and developed loyalty to a set of ideas that confronted dominant ideologies. Ideas such as the need to pay attention to your class position in society, to challenge racism, to rise above your circumstances and never forget where you came from. Our communities have always created culture and knowledge, which effectively counters the mainstream hegemony, which is *counter-hegemonic*.

> **NOTE:** Counter-culture that speaks to the lived experience leaves traces everywhere, from Notting Hill Carnival to Kiss FM. These institutions and many more came into being as outsiders to the cultural mainstream.

When Nipsey Hussle raps in the song 'Loaded Bases' about breaking down the matrix I describe previously, and the nuance of the language of those that do, he wasn't talking about traditional language, rather he's talking about language rooted in communities – a 'hood intellect', if you will, where people and communities have developed a critical eye regarding what's going on and are articulating it in a way they see fit. Antonio Gramsci, the Italian Marxist, defines this person as the 'organic intellectual', who punches up from below, attacking the frameworks of the dominant hegemony. We all need to become organic intellectuals. Global artists, such as Little Simz, Burna Boy and Kano, are prime examples of this for me. Parts of their music – the albums *A Curious Tale of Trials + Person*, *African Giant* and *Hoodies All Summer*, in particular – take a deep, critical look at their subjective, community and national experience and reflect back what they see, with emotion and rigour. In this kind of 'counter-hegemonic' work, we can find not just a voice for our grievances, but also revolutionary thinking. We can find a language that helps us with naming the system, examining life and seeking out ideology, activities that often tend to be contained within academia. But intellectual traditions can also be part of our experience as working-class people at the sharp end of these ideologies; it's part of our legacy, and some of the most incisive revolutionary thinking comes from our communities.

EDUCATION AS LIBERATION

As with many people who grew up as I did, I remain in a constant battle with an internal shadow that makes me believe I'm not capable of doing intellectual work. My shadow has a face, and the same wry smirk as my maths teachers, who laughed at me for suggesting that I might try to make it to Oxford or Cambridge University one day. It is often the case that the 'few' – we as a society class – and 'intelligentsia', those who hail from elite universities, are completely divorced from the 'many', and yet they go on to become the architects of governmental policies that often decimate working-class lives and maintain the status quo. This must be challenged. I believe in working-class intellectualism. I believe it is damaging that we are not taught to collectively come together and analyse the terrain of our lives, to notice how class, race, sexism, homophobia and ableism operate. But also, on a global scale, how imperialism and global capitalism operate.

Every one of us under the yoke of capitalism is in some respects an intellectual in the making, and every one of us interested in changing the world must come together and nurture a fully fledged mass rise of working-class intelligentsia. One which calls out the injustice of poverty wages and racist immigration regimes, but which also embraces all the forms of knowledge, those beyond words, those beyond time, an intelligentsia that unifies heart and mind. Intelligentsia shouldn't just be an elite group of people who sit around thinking and reading all day; they can be anyone who seeks to suss the system, to think deeply about the world, no matter who they are.

NOTE: The Brixton Black Women's Group, a bastion of the Brixton community in its heyday, is an important chapter in the history of black political organising in Britain. They started as a reading group and maintained a tradition of collective consciousness-raising. Same for the Organisation of Women of Asian and African Descent and Abasindi cooperative in Manchester. Based out of Moss Side, they ran Saturday and summer school programmes, giving young people access their own culture, and carried out oral

---

> history projects, such as the Roots History Project
> which detailed the life story members of the
> Manchester African and Caribbean communities
> in the 1980s and 1990s.

Culture and art are integral to political education, and Abasindi Cultural Theatre Workshop brought education back into community hands through the arts, creating work from dancing to playwrighting. Through these organisations, some of the most profound struggles against the miseducation of poor black communities have been waged. We need to return to history, the people's history, and look for the revolutionary minds that have defined the course of our collective journey over the last few decades, from Olive Morris[*] to Rosa Luxemburg.[†]

---

[*] Olive Morris was a community activist in South London and in Manchester. During her short life, Olive Morris co-founded the Brixton Black Women's Group and the Organisation of Women of Asian and African Descent (OWAAD). She was also part of the British Black Panther Movement, and the Manchester Black Women's Co-operative and a leading squatters' rights activist.

[†] Rosa Luxemburg was a Polish Marxist, anti-war activist, writer, philosopher and revolutionary socialist, and an

It is also only in recognising the historical origin of current systems of oppression that we can properly begin to understand and, eventually, overcome them.

architect of social democratic thought. 'Red Rosa' spent years in prison because of her opposition to the first world war. Much like Thomas Sankara, she was assassinated by the very people she used to fight alongside with.

CHAPTER 3

KNOW THE PAST

LIVING HISTORY

The internet was my gateway to learning about the past, and I was lucky enough to stumble across the website historyisaweapon.com, where I was introduced to a world of activists and theorists. I began reading Frederick Douglas, Paula Gunn-Allen and Noam Chomsky among others. When my manager went home, I'd discuss politics and music with the Burkinabé security guard, who recommended I watch the documentary *The Upright Man*, about Thomas Sankara, who led the socialist revolution in Burkina Faso. While wiping down tables at the service station, I could see history unfolding on the plasma screen – the Arab Spring was happening, and then, closer to home, the riots. Streams of territorial support officers from outside London lined the parking bays and came in to order coffees and burgers, all as the Met Police announced they had lost control of the city. That summer I came to understand, in Salvador Allende's words, that history is ours, and people make history, and even more so, that people *have* to make history.*

---

* Salvador Allende was a Chilean socialist politician and president of Chile from 1970 until 1973. He was killed in a

One consequence of 'mainstream' history is the erasure of when ordinary people have moved it, often in the direction of freedom. Our job as activists is to make history whole again. As African American writer James Baldwin once noted, 'people are trapped in history and history is trapped in them'.[6] I've learned this first hand.

> **NOTE:** Every one of us contains these histories: they are our collective memory, they are alive in us, our name, our race, our communities, our religions; they are all traces of these memories, they are all traces of history.

FIND YOUR OWN HISTORY

Before I felt confident to even attend my first protest, I needed to keep pushing my thinking, my beliefs. I needed to know myself and know the world. Nothing was more instructive for me than history. Howard Zinn, first and foremost a

---

US-backed coup. Moments before his death, over the radio to the nation, he said 'History is ours, and people make history'.

historian, left me with an important impression: find the people's history, and then, even more importantly, find your own history. I discovered his work in 2010. Sadly, it was also the year he passed away, but I like to think that year we did him proud: turning his slogan 'we are the 99%' into the rallying cry of the Occupy movement.[*]

The Occupy movement had a simple charge – that the big global banks and private hedge funds were plunging the global economy into chaos. Occupy was hot on the heels of both the Arab Spring and the anti-austerity movement in Spain, the 15-M movement, both of which had transfixed global attention. I watched the protests all while I continued to read and learn more about the histories of human struggle. I'd go home and watch videos online of the Occupy protests in Chicago, in Oakland, in New York. I knew that I needed to help it come to London, and that's exactly what a bunch of us did. What Occupy London, an encampment of hundreds, hoped to achieve was simple: we wanted to highlight the hypocrisy of bailing out banks while

* Howard Zinn was a prolific American activist, historian and professor. He wrote about the Civil Rights anti-war movement and the labour history of the United States.

the people had to endure austerity, we wanted to shine a light on the corporatocracy, which finds its genesis in the square mile.

We tabled a new agenda and it got discussed, at length. Hundreds if not thousands of people came through the camp in central London, on the steps of St Paul's Cathedral, and received not just an education but a taste of what it means to fight back. Occupy inspired a generation.

WHEN THE PAST AND PRESENT COLLIDE

There are living markers of Britain's colonial history all over the country. In our streets, our docks and even on our buildings. And sometimes these markers actively impact on the now, as with the tearing down of the statue of slave trader Edward Colston in Bristol in June 2020.

To give another example, three times a year I help facilitate a week-long political campaigning retreat. Like clockwork, as so often at such gatherings, a disagreement was brewing. In this instance, the legacy of the building was being thrown into question, and in particular whether it had a connection to the Atlantic slave trade. Restlessness and curiosity got the better of me, so I grabbed my laptop and started my own digging, looking into the building's history, and after plunging down the rabbit hole of the wealth of the family who once owned the estate, I stumbled across a free online archive, the 'Slave Registers of former British Colonial Dependencies'. I was curious, and typed in my grandma's maiden name. I'd never met my maternal grandmother, as she died when my mum was young, and my mum never knew where my grandmother was from. Nobody was entirely sure; the biggest hunch was that her family hailed from Mozambique and they were brought over as enslaved peoples. I typed the surname and watched the word Mauritius flash up and four names appeared. I opened the records, scrolled up and down, clicking on the name listed as close to where my grandma had lived. A scanned image of a row of columns appeared: name, colour, work, age, height, origin, owner. I wasn't really prepared to see my ancestors listed in black cursive ink some 180 years ago, as property. I looked closely under origin and there it was: Mozambique.

These records had been made in order to document the enslaved population when Britain's part in the commercial trade of slavery came to an end, following an act that abolished it in most of the British colonies in 1833, and it came into affect on 1 August 1834. Mauritius – a lucrative plantation economy – was actually the last British colony to halt slavery. At that time, the union of the United Kingdom of Great Britain was still relatively young – 127 years young – but the institution of slavery had made this newly unified nation extremely rich, and cemented its racial and economic hierarchy in the world. However, in Mauritius, as in many other places, an adjacent form of enslavement and servitude followed abolition, in the form of continued indentured labour, forced apprenticeships and vagrancy laws. But what didn't change, before Britain's ruling in 1834 and after, was perhaps the most prevalent form of enslaved resistance: 'marooning'. Mauritius, as with the island of Jamaica, had large 'maroon' communities – a combination of enslaved people and indentured labourers, who escaped their servitude and sought their own route to freedom.

On a family trip to Mauritius several years ago, we stopped by Le Morne, a rugged mountain and world heritage site standing over the Indian Ocean on the southwest coast. I remember being told about the escapee population and how they would rather jump to their death from the top of the mountain than be caught. Le Morne was a fortress for maroons, and it was home to a fertile resistance against slavery, where hundreds of people from the African mainland, Madagascar, India and South-East Asia built their own community. The mountain is an international symbol of freedom and resistance, and at the peak of the Western slave trade, Mauritius came to be known as the 'Maroon Republic'. As well as shelter in the forests of the summit, the maroons would also instigate raids and attack slave holdings. It was through this piece of my Mauritian family lore that I learnt that a resistant history was actually part of my inheritance. We all have connections to resistant history, in some way, if we seek it out.

PRODUCT OF HISTORY

I spent three months in Mauritius learning more about my family origins from older matriarchs, learning about our culture, language and national history. I began to understand that I am a product of that history. On more than one occasion, I also visited the offices of left-wing political party Lalit, to learn more about the history of political struggle of the island, the labour organising and also the resistant musical legacies, such as the work of Kaya.* Mauritius only gained independence in 1968, so my parents were both born imperial subjects of the British Empire, and for the centuries prior to independence, as we have seen, the small island nation had been exploited by its parasitic 'mother country'. By having its wealth drained, in the form of free or cheap labour and crops, by having no essential industries developed, save for those that served its coloniser, by having the soil and land

---

*   Kaya was a Mauritian musician and creator of 'seggae' music, a style which combines the popular music of the island – sega and reggae.

decimated by aggressive, intensive agricultural works, and, finally, by setting up a collaborator class through a privileged ethnic minority, Mauritius, much like the rest of Africa, suffers from what historian Walter Rodney described as 'under-development'.* And Mauritius, due to being underdeveloped, is over reliant on a tourism industry that sells it as the 'paradise island'. But, behind the paradise-island veneer, are Mauritians stuck in endless cycles of poverty. Community violence, drug misuse and public-health crises are the hallmarks of day-to-day Mauritian life, and wages are abysmal, yet food prices are skyrocketing, and so Mauritians have been emigrating to Europe for decades, in hope of prosperity, precisely because Europe came to them. This is why I was born in England. As Stuart Hall evocatively summed up his relationship with Britain, 'I am the sugar at the bottom of the English cup of tea'.[7] Mauritius is also one of many small island nations especially susceptible to the effects of climate change – a situation for which it

---

* *How Europe Underdeveloped Africa* is a pioneering book, written by Walter Rodney in 1972, that outlines how the continent of Africa was intentionally exploited and strategically underdeveloped by European colonial regimes.

bears practically no responsibility – yet, if we look at the long history of industry, then, ironically, Mauritius' former imperial master, Britain, is arguably one of the countries most responsible for CO_2 emissions.

Sewing together my own history is one of the most empowering projects I've ever undertaken. We all have a piece in the cloth we make as humankind, and our histories are all connected, just as our present struggles are. So, too, are our futures. Part of gaining self-determination begins with taking command of our individual stories, of our history. Particularly as diasporic youth, this re-telling of our stories is fundamental in regaining our sense of historical context. But history is a battleground. Much of the historical literature I found in the local library in Mauritius was written as an account of the island nation as a colony, measuring its agricultural yield and social issues for the British Crown. It made me realise that, as important as looking into history is knowing how to recognise how ideology has guided history's enquiry, that it is necessary to read between the lines and see beyond the ideology and hegemony.

THE LION'S HISTORY

I was in Eskif (Hasankeyf), in North Kurdistan (Eastern Turkey), a short walk from the river Tigris, beside the valleys that would later take me to Iraq. The recent rainfall meant I would have to stay an extra few days at the campsite I had pitched up in. One evening I noticed a small fire, and a couple of men walking around so I decided to go introduce myself. An older gentleman approached me first and asked me if I had eaten, which I had, so he instead invited me to sit and drink tea with them. He paused frequently to translate the conversation and sometimes ask me my opinion. He recounted how local supposed freedom fighters had recently attacked and occupied the Turkish-operated Ilisu Dam and threatened to flood the 12,000-year-old city whose outer boundaries we sat within.

One of the men sat with us was a former freedom fighter, who had been imprisoned in Turkish gulags for eight years. He asked me where I was from, and the older gentleman translated: 'Britain'. Out of nowhere, the other man stood up, agitated; he began shouting and pointing at me. The older man calmed him, sat him down and turned to me. 'The gulags were not good for his mind, he said he hates Britain.' He was shouting how it was Britain and France that came to this region and divided the land, how it is, 'your country that is responsible'. The next morning I walked to the internet café and googled 'history of Kurdistan'. Blocked. 'Kurdistan'. Blocked. After a third attempt, it was clear that rather than the computer, or internet provider being at fault, this was Turkey at work, one of the most censorship-driven countries in the world, which has been behind the disappearing of innumerable journalists, many of them Kurdish, blocking out whole chunks of history.

We must ask ourselves: what stories are passed on from generation to generation? Whose story is celebrated, and whose is ignored, or erased? How much of our history is the story of the victors? Nigerian author Chinua Achebe often used an old Bantu proverb: 'until the lions have their own historians, the history of the hunt will always glorify the hunter'. The history the former guerrilla I'd met pushed me to explore further, to learn of how Sykes and Picot, an Englishman and a Frenchman, between them created the 'Middle East' we know today, of how Turkey had colonised the Kurdish people: it is the 'hunter's history'. At every turn, revolutionary history is being rewritten, or made to disappear, in order to disadvantage oppressed people.

As historian Linda Tuhiwai Smith reminds us in her work, 'history is not innocent'. Most history is the story of the ruling class, how they became powerful, and, as Smith notes, 'how they use their power to keep them in positions in which they can continue to dominate others'.* The history of modern society as we encounter it through school, TV, cinema, radio and so on, its successive twists and turns through feudalism and slavery, through colonialism and capitalism, is the history of the hunter, a history of erasure. The history of how people were hunted as Moors, hunted as witches, hunted as slaves, hunted as maroons and hunted as Native-Americans is largely absent. To deny people their history is to cut the roots from the tree. Far from being momentary, this erasure is systematic.

---

* Linda Tuhiwai Smith is a Māori scholar of education and critic of persistent colonialism in academic teaching and research. She is best known for her groundbreaking 1999 book, *Decolonizing Methodologies: Research and Indigenous Peoples*.

In the late tenth century, the conquest of Al-Andalus (what is today called Spain) by white Christian Europe, which led to the Muslim Moors being purged from Southern Europe, resulted not just in massacre but in the burning of the Library of Cordoba, which contained 500,000 books, at a time when the largest library in Christian Europe held no more than 1,000 volumes. A few hundred years later, the Granada Library, with 250,000 books, would suffer the same fate. In the conquest of the Americas, indigenous Mesoamericans, such as the Aztecs, Mayans and Mixtecs, would also have thousands of ancient codices destroyed. This was less an attempt by Western colonialists to erase a moment of history, and more an attempt to erase an entire history and way of knowing the world, an entire knowledge system. This process is what Puerto Rican sociologist Ramón Grosfoguel* calls an 'epistemicide'. Grosfoguel talks about four key epistemicides across the fifteenth century, which gave birth to the rise of Western European thought

---

* Ramón Grosfoguel is a professor of Chicano/Latino studies at the University of California, and has contributed greatly to the field of decoloniality, which looks at and interrogates the universality of Western knowledge production and its supposed superiority.

and society: the expulsion of Muslim and Jewish populations from Al-Andalus in Southern Europe, the European witch hunts, the conquest of America, and the kidnapping and enslavement of Africans. The purported superiority of Western thought, Western history and Western civilisation emerged at the same time as Western colonisers sought to completely burn from the face of the planet most other knowledge systems they encountered.

However, as historian Howard Zinn wrote, 'the memory of oppressed people is one thing that cannot be taken away, and for such people, with such memories, revolt is always an inch below the surface'.[8] When the *Manchester Guardian* published the full details of Sykes and Picot's secret treaty in 1917, which shared out the imperial spoils of the 'Great War', – Syria, Lebanon, Palestine, Jordan, Turkey and Iraq – between France and England, revolt spread across the regions affected. France and Britain had simply taken these territories for themselves, areas with vast oil wealth, just as oil was becoming the most valuable commodity on Earth.

We all have at least some sense of history. We're taught history at school, and through this we begin to have a 'memory' of world history, but a wholly incomplete one. We learn of pharaohs and kings, but not of slaves and peasants. We learn when European explorers 'discovered' African, American or Pacific societies, but we do not learn of the societies themselves, which existed for hundreds if not thousands of years before they became known to the Western world. When we come to history, we need to do so by challenging our preconceptions of what history is, and seek out the 'lion's tale'. This means study.

EXERCISE: Go to the Everyday Resources section and create a personal study list. As much as possible, try to organise visits - history lives in the land, on plaques, engravings and tombstones. Include towns your ancestors lived in, the places your family visited. History lives orally too, and in local lives so speak to your elders if you can.

History is the place where we can get a real revolutionary education. Revolutionary because it shows us how we've won against the ruling class in the past. From the moment we find a language to when we suss the system out and use history as a weapon of truth, we find that the history of modernity is a history of constant struggle. Just over two hundred years ago, revolutions tore through America, through France and through Haiti and Ireland. Just over one hundred years ago, the revolutions and revolts of 1917 to 1923, in Russia and Germany, all largely socialist or anti-colonial in nature, shifted the global balance of power between the ruling class and the exploited. Ambalavaner Sivanandan, who had great command of the sweep of history, wrote that 'history tells us where we came from and where we are at. But it also should tell us where we should be going.'[9]

Perhaps the most important gift history offers us is an opportunity to believe and imagine, to believe that a better world is possible and to imagine what that might look like. Historian Robin D. G. Kelley talks about this, calling such imaginings 'freedom dreams', the moments in our collective history where the possibilities of freedom were expansive, where people imagined a world rid of artificial borders, of prisons, of prejudices and exploitation. But as important as what we don't want, Kelley explains that the freedom dreams of the past provide us with fertile soil for nurturing new visions. He explains that 'without new visions, we don't know what to build, only what to knock down. We not only end up confused, rudderless and cynical, but we forget that making a revolution is not a series of clever manoeuvres and tactics, but a process that can and must transform us.'[10]

Learning can and should be one of the most exciting experiences we have as humans; it should awaken what Malcolm X called the 'dormant craving to be mentally alive'.[11] Standardised education numbs the mind, but revolutionary education awakens it. By naming our enemies, sussing out their systems and using history as a weapon, we can prepare our minds and hearts for the work of organising for power and freedom. To revolutionise our thinking is to unbind our minds from the constraints of race, gender and heteronormativity,* to rehumanise one another. Revolutionary education is thoroughly transformative, inside and out. It prepares us not just

---

* Heteronormativity is the dominant belief system that heterosexuality, based on a strict gender binary, is the default and normal sexual orientation. It normalises patriarchal behaviours and societal expectations and denies the multitude of ways that people, relationships, families and communities can exist.

for the struggle, but for engaging our relationships, families and communities with a renewed sense of love and belief in the possibility of change. It might not be 'organising' in the political sense, but it is a radical reorganisation of our mind and heart.

ORGANISE

PLaYLiST

This playlist is selected to invoke growth, movement and community as the energy of our organising. From Tracy Chapman's promise that the poor are gonna rise up to the spiritual powers of the Orishas which Princess Nokia summons in 'Brujas' the songs here remind us that we have all we need to get organised and get free.

Tracy Chapman – 'Talkin' Bout a Revolution'
Nina Simone – 'I Wish I Knew How It Would Feel to Be Free'
Wretch 32 and Avelino, ft. Youngs Teflon – 'GMO'
Joey Bada$$ – 'For My People'
Naughty Boy ft. Ghetts, Bashy, J Spades – 'Do It Big'
Noname – 'Song 33'
Damian Marley – 'Move!'
Princess Nokia – 'Brujas'
Bounty Killer – 'Down In The Ghetto'
Klashnekoff – 'The Revolution (Will Not Be Televised)'
Kendrick Lamar – 'Alright'
The Peace – 'Black Power'
Asa – 'Fire on the Mountain'
Mos Def – 'Umi Says'
Kano – 'SYM'

TRADITIONS OF PROTEST

Britain has one of the longest-standing traditions of organising for power against the ruling class. From the seventeenth-century Levellers to the 1970s–1980s Asian Youth Movements,* as a people we've come together across the centuries to challenge the status quo and strike at the heart of the establishment. At times we have even brought it to its knees. In an age of growing inequality, social divisions and suffering, especially for many marginalised groups, why aren't we fighting back now? Far from being apathetic, perhaps it's because most of us just don't believe in the possibility of political change, which makes sense. Knowledge is key, as I've outlined in the previous section. When most of our radical history is withheld from us, then we simply cannot see how we have succeeded before; without the knowledge of how to climb the mountain, it will always seem insurmountable, which is why it is withheld from us in the first instance.

---

* Anandi Ramamurthy's 2013 book, *Black Star: Britain's Asian Youth Movements*, documents the Asian youth movements that emerged across the country, led by the children of early migrants, who were determined to struggle against both the racism of the street and the state.

As Brazilian educator Paolo Freire famously said, 'There is no such thing as a neutral educational process. Education either functions as an instrument that is used to facilitate the integration of the younger generation into the logic of the present system and bring about conformity to it, or it becomes the practice of freedom.'[1] Education helps us to be political, but that's about as far as it goes. This section is about taking the next step.

We are often reminded about moments in history where people took direct action: the suffragettes planted bombs, and the Civil Rights leaders marched and held coordinated sit-ins. However, direct action is always just the tip of the iceberg. What often gets missed out from the narrative is how people came together, how they built strong coalitions, and how they formulated a strategy. An individual can change the world, but no individual ever really acts alone. To get power, you need people. People to speak to and learn from. People to plan with, and take action with. People to turn an idea into a movement. 'Organise' is about the people, and about finding and building power as an activist. It's about building mass movements. 'People power' is what we need to win back the world.

CHAPTER 4

FIND YOUR PEOPLE

A small sea of signs hoisted above the crowd moved up and down, riding the chorus of chants. I pulled my sign out, and walked across the road with the crowd. My placard was slightly flimsy, held together by lots of Sellotape, and read 'NO MORE TURMOIL'. After a brief pause in the general noise, I took a deep breath and joined in.

The small protest, called by a group called Counterfire, was to demonstrate against the early stages of a NATO military intervention in Libya. I'd come to understand that the 'no-fly-zone' in its early stage was simply a pretence to kill Gaddafi. It was also a way to bring Libya more in line with the international financial regime, which Gaddafi had opposed for decades, as personally he espoused ideas for African sovereignty, and controlled vast gold reserves. The NATO-led intervention I came to realise, was seemingly not in the interest of the Libyan people, so when the opportunity came to protest I knew I needed to get out, join the others and kick up a fuss.

LEARNING FROM EXPERIENCE

I found myself on the steering committee for Counterfire – a socialist organisation and news outlet – attending and on occasion participating in talks on the changing dynamics of the Arab Spring.

Counterfire is arguably one of the most active socialist groups in the country. While I was a member of the steering committee, we began to develop a campaigning organisation, the People's Assembly, which then became the People's Assembly against Austerity, a major actor in the anti-austerity movement, helping to organise marches of up to one hundred thousand people in London, alongside major unions. We had an approach to organising that I wasn't able to name, which I now see was a problem. We rarely talked about what political organising is, and how we should organise, and why we organised with the approach we did. Interestingly, the same issue cropped up when I was an activist within the Occupy movement, the only difference was that there was nobody actively shielding us from that conversation, we just didn't see a need to talk about it. Non-conversation within both groups meant we had a serious lack of a considered approach, strategy or security culture, which, in hindsight, all resulted in people burning out, demands not being met and the group, eventually, fizzling out.

Years later, I was working with some friends on an oral history project and archival collection led by Natasha Mumbi Nkonde and Debs Grayson, called GLC Story. It paired activists of today with people who had done similar work in the time of the Greater London Council, and documents the five years the GLC was run by Labour on a powerful socialist manifesto.* We conducted oral interviews, and our research was exhibited across the city. During that project, I really began to appreciate the need to be clear about the approach to organising I was taking, and, most importantly, what approaches are available.

One of the interviews I conducted was with Brenda Kirsch, who had worked on the Police Committee and Support Unit, and had been very active in trade unions and the Communist Party of Great Britain. Hearing her speak about the publications, the local

---

* The GLC was the government for London before the current Assembly and Mayor. In 1981, the Labour party won control of the GLC on a manifesto that championed anti-sexism, anti-racism, LGBTQIA+ rights, workplace democracy and community-controlled development and embarked on a radical socialist experiment, alongside similar experiments in cities like Liverpool and Sheffield. Margaret Thatcher hated it, and she therefore abolished the GLC in 1986. Find out more on the GLC Story website, http://glcstory.co.uk.

monitoring groups, the information films, working across trade unions, the international campaigns, the setting up of new institutions (some of which still do incredible work today), I began to think about how certain traditions have shaped my own activism, and what approaches are available to me. As a person campaigning around policing at the time, I was inspired to pull back and think about my own approaches in my campaigning. This led me to understand that some approaches sought to advocate for those impacted, and lobby the powerful, while others sought to take direct action, whether through petition or demonstration, mobilising people to make demands from the powerful, and, finally, some sought to organise large organisations with mass memberships, where the people were the power, able to stop the powerful in their tracks. After the interview, I looked back at both Counterfire and Occupy and realised they both actually have quite clear traditions. Organisations, campaign groups and social movements are schools of thought and, like a school, they carry approaches, values and politics generationally; they have genealogies – a line of descent. Extinction Rebellion learned from Occupy, Occupy from Camp for Climate Action, Climate Camp from Reclaim the Streets, and all of these from the school of non-violent direct action that became popular in the anti-globalisation protests of the late nineties onwards.

Identifying and using different approaches and their strategies to achieve your overall aims is one of the key lessons of activism. Finding your approach, however, can be trial and error. At times you'll get it wrong, and every great social movement or local campaign has a story dotted with triumphs and mistakes: the key is to turn it into a lesson.

MOBILISING EFFECTIVELY

My own activism continued with London Black Revs (LBR). As an organisation, we looked at the best black revolutionary socialist approaches of the past, whether that be the Race Today Collective[*] or the

---

[*] The Race Today Collective published the magazine Race Today (1973-1988). The magazines covered the radical anti-racist political organising of the time, as well as cultural events in

Brixton Black Women's Group, and tried to emulate them. When news hit that anti-homeless spikes had been installed to deter rough sleepers across London, LBR took direct action and concreted them over. And, before long, LBR's black-and-red flags could be found at occupied estates scheduled for demolition and at street protests alike. LBR also used direct action to galvanise a spirit of discontent, and we organised a mass 'die-in' at the Westfield Shopping Centre, in the spirit of Black Lives Matter US, who had been protesting the police killing of eighteen-year-old Missouri teenager Mike Brown. Nearly one thousand people attended the 'die-in' and, in a violent mass arrest, seventy-six people were detained and charged by the police. It seemed I'd found my people.

I joined LBR when it was still starting up. The way in which we went about organising – getting hundreds of people out to demonstrate, working fleetingly with local businesses, executing quick, winnable campaigns, focusing on smart messaging

---

Britain and internationally. *Here to Stay, Here to Fight: A Race Today Anthology* (London: Pluto Press, 2019) contains the best contributions from some of the leading writers and activists of the time.

and catching the attention of the press – was representative of the activism that was happening around us, i.e. we employed an approach that is typically called 'mobilising'.

LBR focused largely on demonstrations and protest, as it was about mobilising people out on to the streets, and absorbing more and more members with each demonstration. We worked hard at getting press attention to raise the alarm about the catastrophes taking place around us, whether that was migrant deaths in the Mediterranean or police violence, and used a number of demonstrative stunts to achieve this. As with similar groups around us, we had highly ambitious goals and demands, but, unfortunately, rarely a clear plan or roadmap towards achieving them, save for more protest, more media coverage and, hopefully, more members. Although there was a clear core group of us within the organisation, the supporters we were able to mobilise was a fluid and unknown base. At the time, we had tens of thousands of followers across social media, but they were an unreliable and unknown source of power. All of these characteristics and approaches are symptomatic of a mobilising-driven organisation. Mobilising is perhaps one of the most widely used approaches to political organising, used by campaign groups and non-governmental organisations (NGOs) the world over, such as with the mass mobilisations in Hong Kong that began in 2019. At critical moments in history, this approach has even been capable of toppling governments, but it also has its limitations.

DIRECT INFLUENCE

Since the eighties, there has been increasingly close shoulder rubbing and cooperation between activists and big well-funded NGOs, think tanks, charities and foundations, which has led to a more corporate approach being taken up by some activist groups, one which is best described as 'advocacy'.

> **DEFINITION: ADVOCACY** – is about influencing the decisions of the powerful by lobbying political, economic, judicial and social institutions, often in the form of back room meetings and litigation.

Unlike mobilising, which relies on supporters turning out to demonstrations or signing petitions, advocacy often has little to no reliance on large numbers of people. Corporate campaigns are a good example of advocacy, in that they try to directly influence lawmakers and decision-makers through litigation, pollsters or comms agencies. Business owner and activist Gina Miller taking on Brexit is a great example of this. Make no mistake: advocacy has positively impacted millions of lives by taking to task unjust legislation or corporate practices.

A PLAN FOR POWER?

Fresh air whipped through the van window as I pulled up on to the kerb. We jumped out, and walked back uphill to the nursing home that had become the community organising HQ of Dudley and West Bromwich West. The old nursing home was now a shell, storing huge piles of banded flyers, and a few sofas where we could crash. As chutney rolled down the samosa I'd found in the kitchen, cups of tea were being passed around while we awaited our briefing. The local organiser walked in, and gave us all the lowdown on the local campaign, which areas were at risk, where the data was showing positive gains. For many of us, indeed thousands of us, the general elections of 2017 and 2019 were our first real taste of mass politics and mass-movement building, which tries to involve as many people as possible. For the duration of Jeremy Corbyn's leadership of the Labour Party, there was a new game in town: speaking to people, lots of people. Jeremy Corbyn's Labour Party built a mobilising machine that prioritised the masses, and more than doubled the membership, making it the largest political party in Europe, with their mantra of 'For the many not the few'. I'd like to think that, had they won in 2019, they would've moved from mass mobilising to mass organising, invigorating local politics with real municipalism (changing society from the town council outwards and upwards), and revitalising mass political engagement. However, don't let anyone tell you that parliamentary politics is the only place where mass politics can happen, as mass politics can and should be happening in estates, warehouses, restaurants, supermarkets, schools, care homes and hospitals, through unions and grassroots political organisations.

Talking to people on the doorstep while canvassing, it was clear that there have been many points in British history where it was commonplace to be part of any number of political organisations, be it a union chapter, a community campaign or the local party branch. Nowadays, unfortunately, following decades of the entire political spectrum sliding to the right, this kind of political engagement has all but disappeared, and most people don't see it as a necessity to be part of some kind of political organisation at all. This needs to change.

PRACTICALITIES

When thinking about how you want to organise, which approach suits, the activism you want to do and where you will find your people, the big question you need to ask yourself is what kind of power am I after?

PETITION: If you're seeking to keep a local skate park from being demolished, you may simply need to mobilise for a petition in the community and head down with some of your mates to the local council chambers.

PR CAMPAIGN: If you're seeking to reverse a piece of government legislation, which is harming an already disadvantaged community, you may need to run a high-profile PR campaign, engage sympathetic communities and spend time lobbying politicians and advocating for legislative change, as the amazing feminist organisation Level Up have done successfully.

PEOPLE POWER: If you want to end climate change, you'll need to build people power in the form of high participation and international mass movements, where workers, citizens, students and frontline communities and consumers are organising together and delivering collective action capable of shutting down entire economies.

Of the three major approaches to political activism listed, the last is the only one capable of truly changing the system, because, to provoke a revolutionary situation, you'll need mass people power and mass member organisations ready to show that power.

ORGANISING IN ACTION

I'm a member of the London Renter's Union (LRU), and our organisational goal is simple: to transform the housing system. We see the housing system as rigged to work in the favour of huge land developers and landlords, many of whom work closely with or are in government. We recognise that, to be able to win this huge goal, we need *big* people power. So, as a group, we utilise all three approaches:

1. **WE LOBBY** alongside NGOs for housing legislation to be changed.

2. **WE MOBILISE** members and supporters out to demonstrations.

3. **WE ORGANISE** at the local branch level, with street stalls, door knocking and speaking with the community, building leadership and mass membership.

Organising is always at the heart of our approach at the LRU, and this is symptomatic in the following ways. As a union, we take a multi-issue approach and see housing as intimately connected to immigration regimes, and health, criminal and climate justice, to name but a few – this is emblematic of mass member organisations, whose members face multiple issues in their lives and can't afford to fight in siloed struggles. We have a growing member and supporter base who are reliable, and able to mobilise for urgent needs, such as an eviction. We focus on recruiting new members, especially those at the sharpest end of the housing crisis – the working class – and, if they are interested in fighting back against evictions, and the system that enforces it, we give them training and resources to help them develop into organisers, activists and community leaders. We operate in the communities where we live, empowering people to understand further the political context to their individual crises, providing a political home from where they can be protected and fight for others.

Organising is about moving activism from the marginal into the heart of the community, city and everyday life. The people power that this type of organising wields is normally executed in the form of mass collective action, such as the withdrawing of rent, labour or purchasing power. It is mass organising that won many nations' independence from European imperialism in the first half of the twentieth century, just as it is organising that won universal suffrage and the eight-hour working day.

It's important to stress that these approaches are not just capable of co-existing, but are stronger for it, and different historical movements have demonstrated the ability to wield one, two or all three approaches effectively.

THE BIG THREE

Across the Atlantic, human rights activist Ella Baker* and her co-organisers across the Civil Rights movement, including Dr Martin Luther King Jr, utilised *organising* traditions to cultivate strong political leaders, able to bring large communities into their political agency by talking to lots of people. Through organising, they were able to run tight campaigns that sought to *mobilise* tens of thousands out to vote, protest or petition. Dr King himself *advocated* directly with the President at the time Lyndon B Johnson. It is the success of all three – organise, mobilise and advocate – that created a mass movement. Mass is an important word. Campaigns and organisations that are effectively, intentionally activating multiple approaches of

---

* Ella Baker was a furtive organiser, who played a crucial role in establishing some of the most influential Civil Rights organisations today such as the NAACP, Southern Christian Leadership Conference and Student Nonviolent Coordinating Committee.

building power, towards mass participation, will change the culture of politics and society, and will undoubtedly change the world.

WHERE ARE THE WORKING CLASS?

The more I've found myself in the activist world, in left-leaning social movements and in the orbit of small-to-large NGOs and charities, the more I've begun to feel like the whole space has an aversion to working-class people, and especially ethnic minorities. The simple truth is these groups are as underrepresented in activism, NGOs and charities as they are in mainstream newsrooms, academia or government. There is no doubt that, if you're interested in changing not just a local policy, but the whole corrupt system, you need to think about how the people impacted are getting involved. When thinking about how this happens, we can look at great examples around the world today, from the Awami Workers Party[*] in Pakistan to the

---

[*] The Awami Workers Party is a political party in Pakistan which formed from a merger of three left-wing parties in 2012. The AWP organises dispossessed communities such as low-paid workers, peasants and ethnic and religious minorities toward a democratic and socialist system.

Chicago Teachers' Union in the USA and Abahlali baseMjondolo in South Africa.

One of our local branch coordinators at the LRU said something about organising that stuck: 'things only change when we hit the roads'.

WE NEED TO:

1. Hit the road and meet people where they are, in order to be organisers that are around, reliable and part of the conversation wherever it is that we need to be building power.

2. Remind people that it is only by being part of a political organisation, by being present in numbers, that we can transform the system.

3. Build power, and then test it and assert it by again hitting the roads, whether that's in a protest, for a march or picket line.

The approaches discussed here, and the historical examples available to us, *work*: they are tried and tested, they build power, and power is what we need, so learn them and use them. As political activists on the left, we operate in a vibrant and thriving market of political traditions and approaches. To really organise with intention, we need to find an approach that feels right, and we need to be conscious about how we're choosing to build power and who we're doing that with; you need to find your people. It's too easy to become a cog in the wheel of somebody else's political machinery, and throw coal into the fire without ever being shown the blueprint of the furnace. While, there's nothing wrong with being a cog, as we all need to be one at some point, a lot of us end up getting lost in the bigger machinery, working on plans we had no say in, and might not even really believe in. Nothing is worse than inadvertently being part of other people's traditions, working hard and then realising you don't believe in power being built that way.

CHAPTER 5

FORM a STRATEGY

They say American abolitionist Harriet Tubman[*] used to carry two chickens with her on the riskiest scouting missions when she returned down South. If a slave owner saw her roaming their plantation, she'd drop one, keep the other under her arm and make out like she was chasing it, before making a break for it. The slave owner would watch on in bemusement at an old black woman being outrun and outwitted by a chicken. Yet, in truth, Tubman was the complete opposite – a powerful orator, a firm believer in human freedom *and* a masterful strategist. After years spent freeing enslaved people, Tubman was the first woman to lead a military campaign in the American Civil War, planning and executing the Combahee River Raid in 1863, where she rescued more than 750 enslaved people. After numerous scouting missions and careful strategy sessions, she made her move in the dead of the night with a battalion of 300 black soldiers on three steamboats down the Combahee. On landfall, they torched the plantations and sounded

[*] Harriet Tubman was an American abolitionist, military strategist, nurse, spy and political activist who is well known for her extraordinary work freeing slaves with the Underground Railroad.

a whistle – freedom's call – through the still night air. The powerful would rather have you think that these courageous acts of defiance just happened, but they never 'just happen': they are the product of careful strategic operations.

It's Tubman's legacy of perseverance and strategy that lived on decades later in the Black Alabama Communists of the South, organising from The Croppers and Farmworkers Union (TCFU). During the Great Depression, and amidst a backdrop of extreme racial violence, black sharecroppers and the Communist Party combined forces and fought back against 'tenant' farming, a new working structure that essentially kept intact the power relations of slavery. Looking at their social situation, the strategies were clear: 'Call mass meetings in each township and on each large plantation. Set up Relief Councils at these meetings. Organise hunger marches on the towns to demand food and clothing from the supply merchants and bankers who have sucked you dry year after year [. . .] Join hands with the unemployed workers of the towns and with their organizations which are fighting the same battle for bread.'[2] These legacies of black organising in the South – considered, strategic, mass mobilised – were the precursor to what came decades later: the Civil Rights movement. All these movements, from the abolitionist Underground Railroad, the black Communist sharecroppers to the Civil Rights organisers, all recognised that they had to out-strategise their opponents.

When it comes to activism, we tend to only learn about the products, the protests: Martin Luther King marched through Selma, the Suffragettes went on hunger strikes, and protestors took to social media in the Arab Spring. What we don't learn is the strategic organising Ella Baker undertook with ordinary students, forming the Student Non-violent Coordinating Committee (SNCC), arguably turning the tide for Civil Rights in America; how Sylvia Pankhurst organised with working women of the East London Federation to build power toward winning not just women's suffrage, but also better working conditions; or how revolutionary neighbourhood committees organised within the Syrian revolution, mosque by mosque, before the civil war. There are very, very few examples of strikes, revolts or direct actions of any kind that can claim sweeping success that didn't have a bedrock of carefully considered strategies, as simply employing tactics without strategy is a sure-fire way to *not* win and achieve your goals. As my social justice training mentor and friend Nim Ralph often reminds budding campaigners, many groups fail because they are tactical rather than strategic.

There is danger in having no strategy. With Occupy London, we accomplished many things: we kept the hypocrisy of bailing out bankers but punishing the poor high up the political agenda; we shone a light on the murky activities of financial centres; and, importantly, the encampment was a living, breathing exercise in direct democracy and direct education. However, like many activist movements, it grew inwards as opposed to outwards. One thing Occupy London was not was strategic, and nearly none of its demands were met.

Without a clear strategy to win its demands, Occupy became simply a sprawling, highly powerful tactic: occupation, in this instance occupying London's central financial district. But a tactic can never substitute for a strategy. Tactics service objectives, objectives service strategies, and strategies service goals. Looking back at that transformative time, I can see how, with a strategy, a clear plan, a sense of political tradition and some structure, Occupy could have transformed the political climate, and remained a functioning, powerful movement and organisation.

FORMING A STRATEGY

Marshall Ganz was the organiser-in-chief behind Barack Obama's 2008 Presidential campaign. The grassroots organising and training strategy the campaign used, Ganz learned from the very same students that Ella Baker organised. He summarises strategy as: 'turning *what you have* into *what you need* to *get what you want*'.[3] This means that you have to have a clear understanding of your goals, but also of your resources, alliances, opportunities, constituents, objectives and tactics. Equally importantly, you should have a clear understanding of your opponent's goals, their alliances, constituents, resources and so on. There are many, many ways to form strategy, and, depending on where you are with your approach, it may not need to be overly complex. The fundamental objective with any strategic planning is to figure out what power you need, where it is and how you get it. There are broadly two categories of power: power over (distributive power) and power with (collective power). We tend to only understand power as power over, as that's the one that most affects us, but activism is about the recognition and consolidation of collective power. So, when you're doing your strategy exercises, make sure they also look at the power and influence we have.

There's a whole array of strategy-planning activities that can help with getting 'what you need', from *spectrum of allies* and *power mapping*, to more complex ones, such as *power structure and content analyses, theory of change design, action stars,* and *concessions vs disruptions measurements.*

POWER ANALYSIS

US Labour organiser Jane McAlevey wrote in her article 'It Takes a Community' about an organising approach in Connecticut that tied community organising and union organising into a highly effective approach. This approach ultimately won 4,500 new work contracts, providing huge improvements to pay, healthcare, childcare. The group also stopped four housing estates from being demolished, won $15 million to renovate those estates, got the first African-American woman on to the school board and the first Latin-American person on to the city council. As McAlevey explains, all of this started with a power structure analysis (PSA).

The PSA Jane McAlevey uses, was first developed by community organiser of thirty years Anthony Thigpenn. This PSA is about having a map of how power operates around your goal. It's simply identifying 'the real power players in a given community, or area, determining what the basis of their power is, and finding out who their natural opponents and allies are'.[4]

EXERCISE:

1. On a big sheet of paper chart the world that exists around your target, try to write out all the major individuals and organisations they work with, who hold influence over them and whose support they rely on e.g religious establishments, elected politicians.

2. Add in the major individuals and organisations connected to us that can strengthen our

---

> campaign: this could be anyone from a council
> member, a tenant's association, a community
> centre, or a charity.
>
> 3. By the end you should have multiple nodes
>   coming out which show the terrain of our
>   campaign, and the many avenues to disrupt and
>   put the pressure on your opponent.

It's often the case that our primary targets are unreachable, or refuse to engage with us, so this is why knowing second parties allows us to have secondary targets, which can then apply pressure to your primary targets. Knowing all the different players also allows you to figure out the best tactics down the line, as some nodes might require a back-room meeting, while others might require direct action to feel the pressure of your demands.

INVENTORY ASSESSMENT

Campaign strategies are won and lost on an honest appraisal of resources and capacities. Remember: strategies are fundamentally about one thing – plausibility. At best we'll begin to see exactly how we can win from where we are, at worst we'll begin to see where we need to go and what we need to do to be able to win in the future.

EXERCISE: This exercise is drawn from the Midwest Academy Strategy Chart. Write up three themes: resources, weaknesses and strengths. Hand out post-it notes to all those in attendance, or digitally, and go through each of the following questions one by one, giving people adequate time to think, offer forward and then discuss as a group.

1. **RESOURCES** - What resources are we bringing as an organisation/group? This could be things like money, number of staff, facilities, reputation, communication channels, online resources, local knowledge, political connections.

2. **WEAKNESSES** - What internal weakness are we currently facing, or might we be facing over the course of this campaign?

3. **STRENGTHS** - In what ways do we want to come out of this stronger as an organisation/group? Be as clear as possible, your aims could be: raising money, building a membership base, increasing leadership experience.

SPECTRUM OF ALLIES

A spectrum of allies is a simple chart that allows us to understand the sections of society we're trying to shift in a campaign effort.

EXERCISE: Begin by drawing a semicircle and dividing it into five. Name each segment from left to right:

1. **ACTIVE ALLIES** - Generally those people who are doing things in support of your demand.

2. **PASSIVE ALLIES** - Are those who are sympathetic but are not taking action.

3. **NEUTRAL** - Tend to be groups who may not know anything about the situation or demand and don't have a strong opinion either way.

4. **PASSIVE OPPONENTS** - Are not sympathetic and feel oppositional to your movement or demand but are not doing anything with those feelings.

5. **ACTIVE OPPONENTS** - Are those who completely disagree with you and are taking action/would take action to prevent your demand succeeding.

In most campaign situations, we're trying to mobilise popular support, which means we need to shift people active support. The good news is it also means we don't always need to focus on attacking the opposition, as we may just need to focus on the passive opposition, or on activating the passive allies into action. Working from the main demand of your campaign, begin to fill in each wedge with names of people, groups and organisations.

When filling in each segment we need to be super specific about the constituencies. The more specific we are, the more useful it is when we're thinking about how we move people into action. So, not just 'students' but students *where*, which *type* of students etc. Not just members, but members *where*, and *which* members. Not just 'unions' but which sector, which unions specifically, and which sector of the membership! This is really important, as some of these will form our targets, where we focus a lot of energy and resource.

DISRUPTIONS VS CONCESSIONS

A key process at work in most disputes is what social movement theorist Joseph Luders, a professor in the Political Science department at Yeshiva University, calls 'disruptions vs concession costs'. Many people look to the Civil Rights era as an example of civil disobedience at its greatest, and rightly so. Social movements and activists often point to the mass arrests, the sit-ins, the boycotts, the marches and the voter drives as an example of how, as the Industrial Workers of the World (IWW) says, 'direct action brings the goods'. But Luders suggests that, beneath the surface, there was actually, location by location, a tug of war between disruption costs and concession costs. When disruption exceeds concession, you have a higher chance of winning. This often intricately revolves around third parties: it might be voter bases or customers. Patrick Jones, when reviewing Luders' theory, added that concession costs are also contextually important. If a business is launching a new product, if a politician is going for re-election or wants to pass legislation, this is when they are most vulnerable to disruption targeting third parties.

The anticipated losses through reputational damage can never be understated and the high-cost work of the Israeli state in countering the international BDS (Boycott, Divestment, Sanctions) movement is testament to this. The third party is a key constituency in any struggle and good power structure analysis is a great way to map out third parties.

EXERCISE: The key questions you should ask are:

1. **WHAT** are the concession costs to the power holder if they concede to our demands?

2. **WHO** are the third parties that open up vulnerabilities to increased losses? This might be in the form of economic loss, influence, or allegiance.

3. **DO WE** have the power needed to ramp up disruption costs to higher than the concessions, or close?

START WITH THE VISION

Fifteen or so of us were sprawled across the conservatory of a countryside home we had borrowed for the weekend. The person leading the session handed out some pens with pretty clear instructions – draw it. Prompt by prompt, we were asked to work out the world we wanted to see, visually. The sun still shining outside, food stewing in the kitchen, the group absorbed in the exercise at hand, I felt like we were doing exactly what we needed to be doing: envisioning. As a climate justice organisation, we began to coalesce on a vision of global reparations that could map on to the political conversations around a 'Green New Deal'.* We dreamt of organising within our communities, and especially with young people. A strategy starts with a goal, a vision. But it's important

---

* First proposed in 2008, 'The Green New Deal' is a bold plan to transform almost every aspect of our economy and society in order to tackle both the climate crisis and the social crisis. In particular it proposes huge government intervention to restructure our economy by creating millions of well paid, secure 'green', i.e. environmentally friendly, jobs.

to differentiate between an organisational goal and a campaign goal.

ORGANISATIONAL GOAL – This is the overall goal of your organisation or movement. For example, this could be ending the Conservative Party policy of the Hostile Environment for migrants and asylum seekers.

CAMPAIGN GOAL – Campaigns are the smaller battles you wage to build confidence, win concessions, fight urgent battles and, ultimately, to come closer to achieving your overall goal. A campaign goal in relation to an organisational goal might be winning the right to work for migrants.

The Black Panther Party always had the overarching organisational goal of revolutionary socialism, of winning 'the power to determine the destiny of our black community', but their first campaign goal, in contrast, was to address the number of road accidents and install a traffic light in downtown Oakland. It's also important to differentiate between goals, objectives and tactics.

> **NOTE:**
>
> **GOALS** are the big overall desired wins: it's the final score that you want.
>
> **OBJECTIVES** are the measurable steps you hit to achieve the goal, a bit like mini goals.
>
> **TACTICS** are the methods you use to pursue your objectives.

The LRU had a campaign *goal* of the government scrapping no-fault evictions, and one *objective* was to win over key politicians, while the *tactics* we used to do this were letter-writing and pressure through social media. Along with the rest of the coalition, we won that goal.

As with both examples, the organisational goals are visionary. They need to be, as we have an absence of visions, and this is where we can return to the notion of 'freedom dreams'.

> **NOTE:** Robin D. G. Kelley writes about Freedom Dreams as the moments in the past where the Black Radical Imagination focused on the question

> of what kind of world we're fighting for. Freedom
> dreams call on us to cast a vision of what we're
> fighting for that is born of this moment but that
> looks to the best of the past for inspiration.

Whether we're trying to set up a local newspaper,
end the military industrial complex, or achieve
revolutionary socialism, we need to exercise our
imagination. That creative place where head, heart
and history meet.

EVERYONE IN THE WAR ROOM

There's often another question mark when it comes
to strategy and planning: who should be doing it?
As long-time US union organiser Jane McAlevey[*]
stresses, the *you* in Marshall Ganz's quote – 'turning
what you have into what you need to get what you
want' – is very important. I've been part of plenty of

---

[*] Jane McAlevey's *No Shortcuts: Organising for Power in the New
Gilded Age* is a very useful and inspiring, albeit technical,
book about the traditions of organising and how to create and
apply good strategy. McAlevey's article 'It Takes a Community:
Building Unions from the Outside In', is also very instructive
in thinking about what community-driven strategy can look
like.

groups and organisations where, internally, we had very different appetites for what we wanted, and very different perspectives on the lay of the land, often based on our different social experiences. We all have different backgrounds, networks and aspirations, after all. The lesson here is to always let strategic work be guided by the widest section of people in your organisation or community.

Absolutely everyone should be involved in planning. Strategic planning, which guides groups and organisations, is not best left to consultants, specialists, activists, staff or otherwise. You do want political experience in the strategy room, but you also want lived experience of the issues we're tackling, or of the communities where we're organising. This also means that serious consideration should be given to how different people can get into the room: is there a budget for a crèche worker? Can we cover people's travel expenses? Can we spread it across evenings and make sure to prepare food?

Strategy, like activism, is not a race. The key to success is actually pace. The fight for freedom and emancipation from a rigged economic and political system is a four-hundred-year struggle that has taken many forms, so if it takes months to figure out how your group will win, and the environment changes so it takes a few weeks more, then that's what it takes. Just as you wouldn't expect to win in any other arena without a plan, political organising is the same: we have to out-strategise our opponents. The great news is that our secret weapon is something they simply don't have: the people. Our experiences, charisma, intuitions, millions of connections, our labour, our power, is what is made available through careful strategy.

KEEP IMPROVING

Finally, *debriefing and evaluation is key*. However you choose to do it as a group, make sure you factor it into the strategy. It is arguably one of the most important, yet most often forgotten, elements of political organising. Monitoring and evaluation is important in order to understand your strengths, weaknesses and how you can keep improving, so make sure you factor it into the strategic planning.

Resist & Renew are a collective of radical educators based in London, who have several years' experience running participatory trainings and retreats for grassroots activist groups, NGOs and charities.

One of our flagship workshops is called 'Exploring Collective Liberation', a multi-day retreat aimed at exploring questions of race, power, oppression and how we can get free collectively. The first time we ran the retreat for twenty people, for people from across the country, was a big challenge. From food to accommodation, curriculum to travel, we met various obstacles and made mistakes.

The retreat was a success, but it was not without big takeaways about how to do it better, and we were only able to understand these ways through monitoring and evaluation. There were two major ways we used monitoring and evaluation to improve the delivery and quality of future retreats; firstly, we carried out a daily debrief session, where we used pre-designed questions to reflect on the strengths and weaknesses of the day, and how the remaining days could be improved: this was our form of monitoring. The evaluation came a few days after the retreat, where we went step by step through each day, each activity, and reflected on things like the flow of each day, and then the flow of the overall week. We analysed the feedback we'd received from participants, looking for pieces of information on the impact, and how we can improve for the future, and we reflected on our daily debriefs.

CREATING OPPORTUNITIES FOR LEARNING

Evaluation is about learning and improving, and in many ways we do it all the time informally when we assess our successes and our mistakes, either as individuals or organisations, and decide to do better in the future – we're constantly evaluating our own actions, but in an organisation we can't afford to miss an opportunity for improvement. Building a culture or system of evaluation into our organisations makes it possible to notice a lot more – the good, the bad and the ugly – and makes for much more useful learning. Feminist direct-action group Sisters Uncut, who over several years have helped build a powerful movement in opposition to government cuts for domestic violence services, always reflect on and evaluate their direct-action protests immediately after they have taken place. This practice has led to continual improvement in how they outreach and carry out their protests, leading them to be more inclusive and more safe.

Monitoring and evaluation can be as simple as the above, i.e. debriefing as we go or, providing evaluation forms for the people we work with and doing a thorough evaluation at the end. When we build in a culture of talking openly about our mistakes as we go, of monitoring our outputs, when we evaluate in a participatory way, we can improve the yield and quality of our *outcomes* – the changes we are seeking to make with our organisations and movements – exponentially.

Evaluation also produces accountability, not just to ourselves and our goals and objectives, but to the wider communities we organise with and within. Through monitoring and evaluation, we can begin to honestly answer the question: is our activism improving the lives of the people we're trying to empower and uplift in the way we want it to? Evaluation does not need to be a dry exercise, it can and should be a participatory and empowering part of the work, it can be done through games and interviews, and by training people who wouldn't normally conduct evaluation to learn about and take responsibility for it. Having a person who volunteers to take responsibility in ensuring monitoring and evaluation takes place is a simple way to ensure it gets done.

In activism, there tends to be a lot of work that goes unquestioned, and rarely a moment to pause and ask: *Are we reaching the people we need to? Are we having the impact we need to be having? Are we providing the resources/services etc?* In the reverse set-up, there are many civil-society organisations that spend far too much time and money on monitoring and evaluation, hiring expensive consultants, focused on proving or disproving a very narrow definition of 'impact'. The main point for us is about being accountable to ourselves and the communities we're seeking to build power with and doing honest evaluation so we can continually improve. How we approach monitoring and evaluation should be flexible and context specific, as the point is simply: do it.

CHAPTER 6

GET STRONG

I was fortunate to live in a house once we left the council block even though it was a bit of a wild house. We settled into that small bungalow and eventually made it into a home. My family was a unit, and love and generosity were at the heart of our life, but it was also held together by a culture that was dysfunctional in a lot of ways. My father, for all his virtues and vices, hails from a line of men who have endured challenging circumstances that have changed them for better and for worse. My mother, meanwhile, the hero that she is, hails from a long line of women who have led families but toiled hard; housework is the unpaid domestic labour that makes the world go round, that revitalises us and allows us to conjure up the strength to work every day. Their relationship has, in many ways, been an endurance test. As with most families, we reproduced many of the ills of wider society within our home, such as the normalisation of mistreatment and violence, or the reproduction of gender roles, where reproductive and emotional labour is divided so that women bear the brunt. Over time, we have begun to work these things out, slowly, because the love is there, but that is not always the case for the communities we live in, and the communities that we forge with our political work. I mention all this in order to demonstrate that we also bring our lives with us into our activism, our upbringings, our traumas, our privileges, our fears, our prejudices, our stigmas, our carelessness, our distrusts, our addictions and our anxieties. This shows up in a number of ways: how we hold each other to account, or don't; how we make our groups exclusive or inaccessible; how we overwork and burnout; and, finally, how we leave ourselves open and unprepared for the police and the surveillance state.

ORGANISATIONAL CULTURE

Forming a strong group culture strengthens the heart of political organising; it is make or break. The new cultures we create within our political groups and organisations are an opportunity to practise resistance with the values we wish to see practised in the future; values of healing, of sustainable work, of forgiveness, of humanising one another, of diverse leadership, of creativity.

Many political movements are like families, in that there's an outward story that's being told, and another more intimate story, which often gets written out of history. This often means that the mistreatment of women in the Black Panther Party by fellow male members is forgotten, or that the disregard the mainstream union movements showed for racialised workers organising against their bosses, as seen in the 1974 Imperial Typewriters Strike in Leicester,[*] is ignored. As much as it was state violence that eroded the powerful political movements of the 60s, 70s and 80s, it was also undoubtedly the internal cultures of some of these organisations that tore a hole of injustice into the fabric of their work, and often left oppressive men in charge. This reproduction of everyday violence, internal racism(s), and depoliticisation of the division of labour happens all the way along the line, from the national political party to the local student group. In how we need to think about this, the iconoclastic, black feminist socialist Combahee River Collective put it succinctly: 'In the practice of our politics we do not believe that the end always justifies the means'.[5] This means that

---

[*] Upon realisation that their white colleagues were paid more, and already facing poor working condition, 39 workers at Imperial Typewriters, mostly South Asian Women, decided to take industrial action and were soon followed by several hundred workers. The strikers faced arrests, threats from the far-right National Front and importantly, gained no backing from their union, the local Transport and General Workers' Union. You can find further information and materials to watch at https://strikeatimperial.net/

what we're hoping to achieve can never be more important than how we hope to get there, as both are crucial, and if our practise is liberatory and not oppressive to one another, we are more likely to reach freedom.

A clear sense of the approaches available to you, a vision, strategy, an organisation: these are all foundational elements of what it means to engage in political activism. But to build resilient and inclusive organisations, there are important lessons to be learnt, which movements of the past have taught us, that we often fail to put to work. Outside of the moments of crisis, strong organisational culture can make the day-to-day work of political organising open, healing and transformative. Burnout, infiltration, lack of thought given to accessibility and inclusivity, no just accountability structure, no recognition of gendered labour, no culture of eating together: these frequent occurrences are all manageable elements when thought is given to them in hindsight. When we allow our groups to develop strong organisational cultures, we transform not just the work, but ourselves. When we don't, we fall apart, often in bursts of flames, as I have seen too often. Thích Nhất Hạnh, the Vietnamese peace activist, says, 'the Sangha* is an island of peace. The Sangha is a community of resistance',[6] meaning that our communities of practice must be like islands of peace, and that, when we make peace happen in our work, then our work truly has the ability to make peace possible.

THE IMPORTANCE OF MAINTENANCE

Wretched of the Earth, or WoTE (pronounced: wotay), is a grassroots collective for indigenous, black, brown and diaspora groups and individuals fighting for climate justice. Wretched of the Earth disrupts mainstream environmentalism: it's about climate justice, which, at its heart, says that economic, racial and social injustice is at the heart of climate injustice, and you cannot separate them. It is also, unlike much of the environmental movement, staunchly anti-imperialist and feminist. This is a tradition that predates environmentalism. WoTE demonstrated leadership at the 2015 march, and, since then, at many events, talks and protests. However, WoTE has also

---

* Sangha is a Sanskrit word used in many Indian languages, meaning 'association', 'assembly', 'company' or 'community'. It was historically used in a political context to denote a governing assembly in a republic or a kingdom.

experienced numerous ups and downs. Operating in a fast-moving environmental movement, dominated by powerful international NGOs with masses of resources, has meant that the group has been pushed to work faster and harder than its means, an environment that many activists tend to thrive in, until they don't, which results in burnout. Organising as a group of people from different marginalised backgrounds, with our own life baggage and traumas, we ran into conflict both internally and externally. It was a strong group, but not strong enough to endure these trials, and so had to pause for many months.

It's no exaggeration to say that the majority of most activist groups and organisations I know do not survive these tests: conflict, overwork, inaccessibility, harm, an absence of security culture. However, in the last two years WoTe, more than most organisations I know, has provided a beacon of hope in how to overcome this. By taking time to consider these gaps in our group practice, by naming the issues and prioritising how to build a strong group culture, we are building a community that nourishes, heals and makes resistance less harmful and more joyful. One of the ways we did this was by creating an internal group responsible for generating and strengthening group culture: we call it the 'Maintenance' group. Maintenance is born from the understanding that a group needs to be maintained, and that, when we aren't conscious about that fact, the work of maintaining a group can become absent, or as is most often the case, it becomes gendered, racialised and classed, i.e. poor people consider the upkeep, while more affluent people consider the strategies. Another common occurrence is that the work of reproducing the group itself, socially reproductive work, such as the cooking, cleaning, childcare, frequently gets gendered, i.e. women do a lot of it. Maintenance in WoTE went a step further and explored what political values were needed to define our new group culture. There are two key values we settled on: *abolitionist* and *accessible*.

DOING THE WORK

We shuffled through the hotel lobby and toward the plush restaurant overlooking the River Thames. A well-dressed gentleman let us know that the person we were here to see would be coming to join us shortly. Most of the Black Lives Matter UK core team were able to make the meeting, but not all of us, and we'd also invited friends from other organising communities. Who were we waiting for? Angela Davis, a gift to humanity, with her tireless determination and commitment to revolution and personal transformation, an inextinguishable torch of hope in a dark world. We spoke with her at length about community accountability, and she explained what being an abolitionist meant to her: doing the work. The 'work' means studying abolitionist resources – for example, by setting up an Abolitionist Futures reading group, which you can do online. Abolition, to WoTE, BLMUK and many other activist groups, means a commitment to ending the violence of the prison-industrial system, and the carceral ideology that provides its logic. Davis told us about the work of generationFIVE (gen5), an organisation that, since the nineties, has been working to develop and deliver community-based social justice responses to endemic child sexual abuse from an abolitionist framework, using transformative justice approaches. Gen5 also use these methods of transformative justice in working through domestic and sexual violence in left-wing political movements – meaning they sought transformation of parties involved, as opposed to the punishment and disposal of both victim and perpetrator to the vice of the criminal justice system. If abolition is about the dismantling of the repressive apparatus of the state, be it police or prisons, then Transformative Justice is the discipline that gives us alternative methods for resolving conflict and harm that don't simply punish, disappear and even kill our problems. Davis made it clear that this approach requires deep political commitment to learning and trying, but the ultimate reward is that we can potentially really make prisons and police obsolete.

NOTE: Following the George Floyd Uprising protestors and activists in the US and UK, knowing that they confront an issue endemic to the police and criminal justice system, have been embracing the movement for police and prison abolition. This has looked like large-scale rallying behind the demand to 'Defund the Police' as well as many others. This new movement in Britain says that by withdrawing lethal tools such as tasers, by scrapping policing programmes which target specific communities, such as Prevent and the Gangs Matrix and by repealing laws that criminalise survival e.g drug, sex work and migration, we can not only scale back harm caused by police but we can divert and prioritise this spending on community health, education and affordable housing.

This carceral logic is not just the violence of police and prisons, but it also means the violence we produce in our personal relationships, families and communities, whether they are overtly political or not. This brings us back to our political groups. In all our political organising, in the communities we organise within, harm will occur, and it will require accountability. However, if we approach accountability from a carceral mindset, then somebody will be reduced to the moment of transgression, punished and often exiled. Yet, if we approach it from an abolitionist mindset, we see beyond the binary of victim and perpetrator, and we see that carceral logic is a predetermining force. Taking leadership from the harmed person, we aim to transform harm into learning, personal rehabilitation and transformation, as long as the perpetrator is willing to be part of a process.

As Angela Davis writes in her 2003 book *Are Prisons Obsolete?*, 'prison relieves us of the responsibility of seriously engaging with the problems of our society'[7] Abolitionist approaches to accountability do the opposite: we engage the wider problems and produce healing and transformation. This is always a process that moves at its own speed, and gen5 is called that because healing, it is said, can take five generations, and it's an imperfect process, which is why Mariame Kaba and Shira Hassan's book on the topic is called *Fumbling Towards Repair*.[8] The work of Kaba, and the work of INCITE! websites, such as transformharm. org, are great resources for learning more about accountability from a transformative justice approach. Conflict can be scary, and harm is triggering and traumatic, so, as a person who has experienced inter-personal and state violence, I don't take the topic lightly, but conflict is often inevitable and it's far better to be prepared, and believe in the possibility of transforming harm and producing healing.

CREATING INCLUSIVE SPACES

Again, Delores asked for people to speak up because her hearing impairment meant that it was difficult to pick up on people's comments, especially amid the background noise of the pub's upstairs room. We were meeting to discuss a long agenda on activities over previous weeks and work to come, and in that meeting it began to dawn on me how easy – and normalised – it is for a group of non-Disabled people to exclude Disabled people. It also dawned on me how, in our political spaces, as in our workplaces, we often recreate the exact dynamics that Disabled people fight against in society. Delores uses a cane because of her mobility issues, and the meeting room in the pub was upstairs. This was not the first meeting Delores had attended, nor the first where she'd raised that the group was not considering her access needs. Yet again, we'd ended up at a pub that was almost completely inaccessible to her. Granted, she'd made the decision alongside us, but we could have arranged a different venue where it would have been a lot more inclusive for her and for others. Whether we like it or not, we had, deep down, settled with the notion that Delores would have to *make do*. But every time we think that people can 'make do', on any level, we signal to Disabled people, and people with other kinds of access needs, that our groups aren't for them.

Delores made it clear that the group had a lot of learning to do regarding creating an inclusive and accessible space for her and others, so we committed to holding more group conversations (in more audible surroundings) with an aim to further understand what being a truly accessible and inclusive group means.

We also discussed how the use of jargon can exclude people, and how assuming people's genders can exclude trans people. We thought through how to pool money to assist in travel costs for people whose class background means they have less access to money. There was so much to consider, and once we'd discussed the kinds of access needs we could and should make adjustments for, we began to make commitments as a group. We researched locations that were accessible for Delores, with no steps, with hearing loops, and committed to talking louder, slower and, when necessary, using a portable microphone.

TIP

Access needs show up in many different ways: sometimes they are related to disability, sometimes class and economic status, and in other cases, cultural upbringing.

DISABLED WITH A CAPITAL D

Before becoming an activist, I had never realised the complexity and nuances of what exactly it means to be Disabled, let alone how Disabled people have fought for their civil rights, many of which we grow up thinking always existed, things like wheelchair ramps on buses or hearing loops in buildings. I'm not a Disabled person, so my learning has come from the generosity of all the Disabled people I have organised with, been educated by, and read work by. This means I'll inevitably get things wrong: the point is that we keep learning and listening. The language and understanding I use here is debated amongst Disabled communities. Like all oppressed groups, Disabled people are not a homogenous group; for some Disabled people the entire concept

141

of striving for 'inclusivity' reinforces that the 'norm' and standard is still that of a non-Disabled person. Disabled people face barriers in society because society isn't built in a way that accommodates their impairments or differences. Impairments might be physical or mental, but it's not these things that further disable people: it's that society isn't built to meet those needs. Society treats these impairments as abnormalities, which suggests that people being different is the issue not the absence of consideration for a wider spectrum of needs.

When talking about Disabled people, it's important to note that this includes people who have many different types of impairments, including people with visible and invisible physical impairments, people with cognitive impairments, people with chronic physical and mental health problems, D/deaf[*] people, neurodivergent people, which includes autistic people and also people with dyslexia, dyspraxia, epilepsy, Tourettes and mental health problems, and many others.

---

[*] The term D/deaf is used to describe people who are Deaf, i.e. sign language users, and deaf, i.e. who are hard of hearing but who have English as their first language and may lipread and/or use hearing aids.

Britain has an incredible history of Disability campaigners fighting back, which reaches as far back as 1890. These movements have long been shifting public discourse, progressing public policy, advancing critical theory, and winning increased civil rights. Movements such as the Disablement Income Group of the 60s, the Disabled People's Direct Action Network (DAN) of the 90s, or current national grassroots campaigning of Disabled People Against Cuts have made an enormous difference.

One of the key messages of the UK Disability rights movement has been 'Rights Not Charity' – meaning equality, not pity. The summer of 1992 saw over a thousand Disabled activists protest ITV's annual fundraiser for Disabled people. The telethon, they argued, played a big role in reinforcing negative ableist stereotypes of Disabled people, such as those of them being helpless and needing pity. Besides the incredible slogan 'Piss on Pity', the overall message of the demonstration was simple, and the same as that of the British Deaf Association one hundred years earlier: 'nothing about us, without us'. Just as we should not expect a group of rich white people to make good decisions about the lives of poor black people, we should not expect non-Disabled people to make decisions about Disabled people's lives. After the telethon, the group went on to become the Disabled People's Direct Action Network and played a fundamental role in the campaigning and mass demonstrations that forced the government to enact the Disabilty Discrimination Act of 1995, nearly twenty years after the Race Relation Act and Sex Discrimination Act. Their campaigning continues today, because, despite the Act, Disabled people still face constant attacks on their rights.

NOTE: In 2016, a UN report found that, through six years of austerity, the government had committed 'grave and systematic violations' of Disabled people's human rights.[9] Disabled People Against Cuts (DPAC) that was established to fight these attacks, which are directly linked to multiple deaths in the Disabled community. These alleged violations include cuts to Disability Living Allowance (now called the Personal Independence Payment) and Employment and Support Allowance.

My personal of organising with Disabled people has been a challenging one, as I constantly question my internal stereotypes, pay attention to the barriers I create and also learn and reflect on the history of the Disability struggle. Sisters of Frida, a visionary collective that creates platforms to support learning, the sharing of different experiences, and enables people to challenge oppression, includes this prinicipal in their manifesto – 'we expect accessibility'. A statement so simple yet impactful shows that it is part of all activists' work to fight against the disabling practices of the wider society, by removing the barriers to access and making adjustments, just as we fight to remove barriers to secure safe housing, or inclusive high-quality education. Our struggles and our liberation are inextricably linked.

TIP

Sisters of Frida have some amazing online resources about how to organise our groups so that they are accessible and inclusive to Disabled people. They work from the social model of disability, which believes a person can have impairments, or different ways of being, but are disabled by the barriers society places on them, hence why many capitalise the D in Disabled.

The use of a capital 'D' for the word Disabled recognises that society creates barriers for people with impairments, it also illustrates a shared identity and community that fights for rights, like many other oppressed groups. These barriers disallow Disabled people from participating on an equal basis and include not just the attitudes (such as people's expectations that Disabled people can't be leaders), but barriers in physical environments too.

DIFFERENT MODELS

When discussing Disability, the social model is often contrasted to the medical model that continues to shape conversations and approaches to Disability today.

SOCIAL MODEL – For our activism, it's important to note that the social model encourages thinking away from the idea that there is something *wrong* with a Disabled person, and reframes the emphasis to thinking about what can be done to *identify and remove barriers*.

> **MEDICAL MODEL** – The medical model suggests
> that 'normal' is not having impairments, that
> disability is a problem with a Disabled person's
> body, which must be fixed, medicalised and
> cured. The medical model itself is derived from
> the Eugenicist model.

There are several straightforward ways in which
you can help make your political activism more
accessible, not just in relation to Disabled people's
access needs but in relation to the variety of access
needs all people may have, which can include travel
costs, childcare, language interpretation; everyone
has some type of access need. Some top tips, based
on the resources section you can find on the Sisters
of Frida website: www.sisofrida.org.

It's also important for anyone chairing or facilitating
a meeting or event to be prepared for the different
ways that people show up, including the trauma
they may bring and the varied ways people engage
in dialogue and conflict.

Inclusivity also means being unafraid of difference,
and not allowing our differences and different

needs to divide us. As self-described 'black, lesbian, mother, warrior, poet', Audre Lorde wrote, 'Divide and conquer, in our world, must become define and empower'.[10] Lorde wrote prolifically on differences, stressing the need to recognise and celebrate them, as to her our differences are actually a beautiful, necessary part of human diversity. Society works to actively disinclude poor people, racialised people and Disabled people. We are not considered the 'norm' or the mainstream, we have to fight to become the norm, and because of this we have a shared struggle, a struggle against the forces of systemic injustice that work to recreate the 'normal' person. This approach to thinking about disability, which shifts from a framework of accessing increased rights to one of justice, where the problem is derived from the entire political-economic set-up of society, is called the 'Radical Model'* and proscribes to the goal of Disability Justice.

* National Arts Charity Drake Music has a great online resource written by social justice trainer Nim Ralph, called 'Understanding Disability', which is a great starting point for coming to grips with how Disability is understood and goes further into the radical model. https://www.drakemusic.org/blog/nim-ralph/understanding-disability/

DISABILITY JUSTICE

Blogger and Disability rights activist Mia Mingus writes in her blog Leaving Evidence that 'as organisers, we need to think of access with an understanding of disability justice, moving away from an equality-based model of sameness and "we are just like you" to a model of disability that embraces difference, confronts privilege and challenges what is considered "normal" on every front.'[11]

A central part of Disability Justice is reflecting on the concept of care. 'Absent or inadequate support and care', as community organiser and friend Tumu Johnson says, 'is a barrier to life', which means that access to support/care is *access* to life. What does this mean for our political activism? If a person has a carer only for the morning, they might not be able to access a meeting in the evening without additional support. Since these are the barriers society places on them, then our groups must take responsibility to remove them. All our political groups need to simultaneously work as 'care collectives', meaning that we collectivise responsibility to meet each other's access needs, whether related to Disability, chronic illness, class or immigration status and more. How can we make sure that anyone who needs support, whether in going to the toilet or in making a cup of tea, gets that assistance? Will we make sure there are funds to pay for the care required, whether it is provided in the group or sourced from outside? Challenging our concepts of care is critically important. As Leah Lakshmi writes in *Care Work*, this approach to care 'is drastically different from most ways care is thought of in the world, as an isolated, begrudgingly done task', instead, mutually aiding one another and sharing the labour of care and support, can be a 'site of pleasure, joy or community building'.[12]

Accessibility is not a tick-box exercise, it's a political commitment to making political spaces whole. Making our organising spaces inclusive is political; it is part of our shared struggle. When one section of society defines how social and political spaces operate, they will end up being exclusive. By making sure everyone is in the room, we'll have the wisdom to ensure our spaces are open, accessible and inclusive, that they are fighting back against ableist systems, and that they are as powerful as they can be. But thinking about accessibility is never a complete process, whether it's people's experiences of migration, or their experiences as a trans person, we will constantly need to push back against exclusionary norms, make adjustments and work to make our politics and political spaces ever more inclusive. It is, of course, impossible to have a completely inclusive space, since there are a huge variety of access needs, and they sometimes compete, but the point is that we must try to remove as many barriers as possible and get as many people in the room as possible, and keep learning.

RESISTING OVERWORKING

I've spent most of my working life as either a customer assistant or a waiter. There are two ways you can go about those jobs, slowly or fast, but, in reality, if you wanted to keep the job, then you needed to be productive, you needed to overwork to be recognised as efficient, and 'valuable'. My first conscious experience of overworking was at fifteen, while doing my GCSEs. I worked in a two floor Chiquito's on the Leisure West industrial park in Feltham for £4.77 an hour, and I used to man a whole section – which could've been a whole restaurant on its own – while making drinks and desserts. The combination of being on the shop floor, oftentimes in back-to-back twelve-hour shifts, needing to pick up overtime to save money, all drove home a culture of overworking. We never work in just one field either. We work *and* study or raise families (another form of unpaid work), or do activism, or volunteer, or all of the above. To survive in capitalism, for the majority of people, is a matter of adjusting to the enforced necessity of not just working, but overworking.

There were days when I used to race through restocking shelves and handling deliveries on the floor or in the warehouse at Marks & Spencer's or WH Smith. There was something so satisfying about getting the work done, something so instinctive about the need to stay proactive, besides it making the time go more quickly. I always knew why I was there, though, and, without hesitation, I piped up one morning as we all moaned about being badly paid. I made it clear that, as nice as it was to work with everyone there, we were all there for the money, end of. I remember one of my co-workers staring at me for a moment. She was one of the more experienced staff. I couldn't quite work out what she was thinking, until she snapped back into the present and replied: 'that's really true'. I think that part of being institutionalised to work is forgetting that we are a *worker*, and *we work for pay*: full, complete pay.

So often, we become the 'complete worker', in that the sum of who we are becomes the sum of what we do. Again and again, I have witnessed the drive to be seen to be active and busy killing political projects through burnout and conflict. The worrying fact, too, is that there is no shortage of space for 'productivity' when engaging in the political work to transform society. There is enough to literally work yourself to death. Therefore, an attitude of sustainable productivity needs to define our approach, otherwise we hit the point of no return – burnout.

At the beginning of this section, I outlined how we carry our life baggage into activism, and overworking is often part of it. We're pathologically driven to overwork, and workaholism is a disease endemic to capitalism. Whether in Black Lives Matter UK, WoTE or the London Renters' Union, there's an ongoing conversation about overworking and the troubling problem is that this societal culture is doubled up in activism, with the guilt and fear that, if we don't work hard enough, we'll decrease the possibility of justice.

And yet tackling an overworking habit in an organisation is simple, and these solutions actually make an organisation able to thrive in multiple ways. Introducing rotation into roles and ensuring there are layers of participation, for example, not just ensures that people don't overwork, but makes an organisation a more nurturing and accessible space.

TIP

In the London Renters' Union, we use rotational roles as frequently as possible. This not only ensures people don't overwork and can take a pause, but it also means that people are able to pass on and learn new skills.

Having layers of participation is absolutely crucial to the survival of any political organisation. It signals that being involved in your group is not just about intense work, it says there are levels at which the work is less time intensive. It also means that people who want to step down from overworking, but want to stay involved, can do so. The other important element is to create a habit of praising and encouraging members, acknowledging that they are overworking, and setting personal boundaries. Just as in personal life, balance is also key.

PROTECT, PROTECT, PROTECT

In the late hours of 8 March 1971, as Muhammed Ali dropped Joe Fraser, over one thousand documents were burgled from a two-man FBI office in Pennsylvania. By the next day, activist group Citizens' Commission to Investigate the FBI ensured that the world knew the full scale of what they had unearthed: COINTELPRO. This was a sprawling FBI programme that devoted unending resources toward surveilling, disrupting and sabotaging the activities of mostly student organisers, communists, anti-war organisers, and Native American, Latino and black power movements in the 1960s and 70s, at times resulting in killings, such as that of Black Panther Fred Hampton. It was a government surveillance and sabotage programme on an unthinkable scale, waging a physical and psychological war on its own citizens. This attitude from opponents to activism is 'arguably an intended effect of state security practices that seeks to discipline and isolate those targeted, spread fear and deter others from dissenting or organising to challenge the status quo'.[13] Nothing has changed. Protecting activism comes with appreciating the scope of your opponent's operation.

BECOMING A TARGET

Dozens of storefronts transformed overnight, police tapes draped the glass, and coverage of the drama began: 'Lush faces calls for boycott as bizarre advertising campaign accuses police of "lying" and "spying" and says they've "crossed the line"', wrote the *Daily Mail*. Lush cosmetics' 'Spy Cops' campaign backfired, as they realised, as many of us who have dealt with campaigning against the police had realised before them, that the police force is a very powerful institution. Within days, Lush apologised and ended the campaign. But were they wrong? From 1968 to 2011, it is alleged that undercover police spied on more than 1,000 political groups in Britain. A huge amount of these were family justice campaigns, families whose loved ones have been killed in police and state custody. More than five thousand people have died in state custody in Britain since 1990. While with BLMUK, I've had the great honour of fighting alongside some of these campaigns in their coalition, The United Families and Friends Campaign. I can't stress enough the importance of looking at the work of UFFC, understanding the gross injustice of deaths in police and state custody, and finding ways to support these campaigns to access justice.

French philosopher and social theorist Michel Foucault, building upon the ideas of Hannah Arendt[*] and Aimé Césaire[†], spoke of the 'imperial boomerang effect'. Writer and researcher Connor

---

[*] Hannah Arendt is one of the most important political theorists of the twentieth century, her thinking covered the subjects of authority, anti-semitism, totalitarianism and humanism.

[†] Aime Cesaire was an Afro-Caribbean poet, politician and author who was one of the founders and pioneers of the negritude movement, which emerged in 1930s in African diaspora, which called for a black consciousness drawn from pride, culture and an analysis of the world drawn from the Marxist Black Radical Tradition.

Woodman has described this as 'A term for the way in which empires use their colonies as laboratories for methods of counter-insurgency, social control and repression, methods which can then be brought back to the imperial metropolis and deployed against the marginalised'.[14] The Met Police, Met Special Branch, MI5, all these institutions were developed in British colonies, and often used in particular to spy on and disrupt opposition to a ruling class; on activists and revolutionaries. As Woodman writes in his article 'The Infiltrator and The Movement', the Met Police Special Branch and MI5 have, over 100 years, worked closely with business groups and government to infiltrate and destroy socialist movements, labour movements and protest movements.[15] Today, the sweep of these police operations is huge, and it is often arguably targeted directly at minorities and activists. It's almost impossible to protect against infiltration, and paranoia can develop very quickly when you are living in fear of it, but our strength is in our numbers, which returns us to the earlier point of the urgency in building mass movements. As Woodman points out in the same article, our strategy should be to 'organize on as open, deep, and broad a basis as possible'. While doing so, protecting against surveillance, infiltration and an absence of privacy is difficult, but very much essential work.

Political activism makes you a target. If your activism takes aim at the powerful, if you're building people power, you will quickly get the attention of the huge security state apparatus. This means, whether you like it or not, you'll need to take up the fight against the creeping surveillance state, which, since the sixties, has regularly made people like you and me some of their primary targets. A surveillance state is a government that utilises mass surveillance in order to maintain control and authority. Whistleblower Edward Snowden's NSA scandal, which blew the lid on how the UK's Government Communication HQ (GCHQ) harvests more personal data (contact lists, emails, phone locations) than the US (which is forty times the size of UK) was so damaging that a Defence and Security Media Advisory Notice (DA-Notice), an official request not to publish or broadcast on a topic for reasons of national security, was threatened in order to warn the BBC off reporting on the story, which was so clearly in the public interest.

When I was forced to leave the central Occupy encampment, because of a heavy-handed injunction, I moved to the Islington-based Occupy Finsbury Square camp, just twenty minutes away. The camp was made up of a few dozen people, all peaceful, both young and old, simply making a point that the banks are getting away with murder. One evening we were made aware of a circular, which was being delivered to local businesses: we hunted it down, found it and sat down to read it. The warning, printed on City of London Police letterhead, informed local businesses that a terrorist organisation was operating in their vicinity – us, the Occupy movement. I called the police whose letterhead it was and asked if they could verify this. They drove down, rolled down the window, made a call, and verified it. It was then covered in the news the next day.[16] The most insidious thing was that, by simply designating us as an extremist organisation, it opened up an entire array of counter-extremism surveillance tools, and possibilities for charges with heavy custodial sentences; counter-extremism tools, such as Prevent, whose effect is to terrorise the Muslim community, a practice that also defines how the Met Police's Gangs Violence Matrix arguably surveils and terrorises black and brown communities.

So, activist 'security culture', the practice of researching and enacting secure processes when organising, can never be understated. As author and activist Aziz Choudry often says on the matter, we have had too many lessons lost, but we have also had many lessons learned, and we need to incorporate them. As an activist, you need to specifically be aware of the National Domestic Extremism Unit set up by the government to monitor people like you and me, and you need to take necessary measures to protect your members, data, plans and resources. This means, for example, not putting any of those into public domains, such as on Facebook or other social media. You also need to be aware of surveillance measures, such as body recordings and facial recognition, which are used at protests, and, most importantly, what you do and don't need to cooperate with under your legal rights.

TIP

Know your rights! There are a number of organisations who can help in respect to knowing your rights as a protestor, including Green and Black Cross and Netpol. To learn more about how the government expands its surveillance apparatus to undermine activists' work, organisations such as Undercover Research Group, Statewatch, Privacy International and Big Brother Watch are great resources.

Knowing that privacy effectively doesn't exist on our personal devices, and strong physical and digital security are not just good practice, but will become essential to the longevity of our movements, especially as governments clamp down further on our dissent, is enormously important. As convenient as Google is for searching, emailing and file sharing, it is well evidenced that, as an organisation, they have willingly cooperated with the creeping surveillance state. Eric Schmidt, executive chairman of Alphabet inc. (Google's parent company) *and* chairman of the US Department of Defense's Innovation Advisory Board, has even stated, in a CNBC interview in 2009: 'If you have something that you don't want anyone to know, maybe you shouldn't be doing it in the first place.' Worrying stuff, if you believe everyone is entitled to at least a basic level of privacy.

TIP

Some people or organisations run their operations and emails from a secure server, such as Proton Mail or Riseup, as opposed to Google Mail, as they are concerned about surveillance.

NO FACE NO CASE

Drill is an explosive music genre that has come to dominate the rap and grime listenership in the last decade. Lyrically, drill often paints a detailed picture of the lifestyles many of the rappers have found themselves in and around as racialised working class young people, often putting particular focus on the violence that sometimes comes with it. Although many musical genres have, over time, contained challenging lyrics, it is often black genres, be it reggae, grime or drill, that end up drawing the worst kind of attention from the state, even becoming criminalised. It has been shown that police pay close attention to the rise of drill musicians, using their lyrics and whereabouts to further criminalise them, hence, in drill and grime, there's a saying: 'no face, no case'. Some people say this can be seen as a necessary measure to take in order to protect your identity and stay safe: i.e. mask up – in music, or in protest. However, it is still perceived as a crime in the eyes of the police. The Met Police are currently the largest police force outside of China to roll out live facial recognition operationally, scanning millions of people. As the group Big Brother Watch notes on its website, in their Stop Facial Recognition campaign, 'this move gives a green light to police forces and private companies across the UK – and around the world – to turn public spaces into biometric surveillance zones.'[17] Facial recognition allows for mass 'faceprinting' without active consent, which provides biometric data that is as useful, if not more so, than its fingerprint equivalent. Just as we would not freely offer up our fingerprints, people argue that we should try not to give away our face.

TIP

It's not just about giving away your face – your data, and your phone/browsing habits are just as important. Detox your data periodically. Encrypt your communications. Browse anonymously using VPNs. Try to keep sensitive messages on secure apps, such as Telegram. Keep organising conversations off social media as much as possible. Social media is great for spreading the word, but that's it. Destroy sensitive information after use. Switch off your locations function on your electronic items. Finally, head over to places such as securityinabox.org and activistsecurity.org and be proactive in developing your personal and group security culture.

HURTLING TOWARDS FREEDOM

The power of a clear approach, a considered plan and a strong group cannot be overstated. Those three elements working in harmony have birthed and destroyed entire empires. They're certainly not easy, but they lay sturdy foundations that can weather the political storms that lie ahead for us. I had no preparation for any of this, no academic or occupational frame of reference, but I figured it out, often with the help of others, and so can you. If the hundreds of thousands of people who read about and are interested in social, environmental or economic justice felt empowered to not just protest, but to get organising and organised, then we would hurtle toward freedom.

Agitation is the bread and butter of political activism, it is the hallmark by which people commonly come to know activism, through protest and direct action, but beneath and behind the best agitation is good organising. We can do a bit of education and go straight to agitation – hell, we may be so angry at injustice that agitation simply follows – but if you want to really transform the system, if you really want a revolutionary moment, you need to organise.

AGITATE

PLAYLIST

This playlist is selected to invoke fire. The songs here are selected to stir to action, to summon strength and freedom in our actions and to never forget, as musical legend Christy Moore reminds us, that we are many, and they are few.

Erykah Badu – 'The Healer'
M.I.A – 'Paper Planes'
Bob Marley and The Wailers – 'Them Belly Full'
J Spades – 'Strength'
Pa Salieu – 'Bang Out'
Nas ft. Lake – 'Revolutionary Warfare'
Akala – 'Malcolm Said It'
The Game – 'Savage Lifestyle'
Little Simz ft. The Hics – 'Gratitude'
Lowkey – 'My Soul'
Sampa the Great – 'Freedom'
Marvin Gaye – 'Inner City Blues'
Kojey Radical ft Shola Ama and Collard – 'Icarus'
Johnny Osbourne – 'Truth and Rights'
Christy Moore – 'Ordinary Man'

What's a rebel without a rebellion? Wherever we meet injustice – on the street corner, in the workplace, on the steps of government buildings – we need to fight. Educated, organised and fighting back, we are undefeatable. For as long as there has been injustice in the world, there has been a formidable struggle against it, exploding into moments of agitation. Agitation – direct action – is our heritage. Agitation is about reversing the crises that the mass of the people has had to endure: the economic crisis, the housing crisis, the health crises, the domestic and community violence crises, the Climate Crisis. During these crises, the rich are continuing to get richer and profiting off the suffering and exploitation of marginalised communities. If we want to end this violation and inequality, we need to create and sustain a crisis for the rich in turn, we need to cause major disturbances. In this section, following on from the skills of knowing yourself and the world, of organising and strategy, I will introduce you to the skills and arguments related to taking action.

CHAPTER 7

GET PROTESTING

We were on rotational sleep shifts at the media hub, trying to stay on top of any emerging security risks and watching the back of the protestors who were cutting their way through the outer perimeter fences. The banner we'd been painting only days earlier in the sunshine was now laid across the tarmac beneath a home-made fifteen-foot bamboo tripod which cradled a person in the middle. Black Lives Matter UK had occupied the runway; London City Airport was shut down. Several hours and 131 cancelled flights later, airport expansion, climate crisis, the hostile environment and environmental racism were suddenly an unavoidable topic of conversation on radio shows and TV programmes around the country. But it was not without heavy costs: 'assassination pieces' hit the press, governmental ministers followed up with questions about our activities in the House of Commons, and the personal businesses of members were targeted and destroyed. Even though it was a peaceful, if disruptive, protest, we were tried and convicted. However, direct action, disruption, crisis, and, most importantly, strategic sustained crisis is how we will win.

DIRECT ACTION

The Oxford English Dictionary definition of 'direct action' is: the use of strikes, demonstrations, or other public forms of protest rather than negotiation to achieve one's demands. It's not entirely correct, as sometimes strikes and demonstrations can be used to force your opponent *into* a negotiation, or to *strengthen your hand* in a negotiation. But, either way, direct action is about taking things into our own hands, asserting our power, disrupting 'business as usual' and creating a direct, sustained crisis for our opposition.

Direct action comes in many forms. After the Christchurch Massacre in New Zealand in 2019, where a white supremacist shooter killed fifty-one worshippers in a mosque, a few of us, as activists from different groups, got together and organised a vigil. We decided to assemble outside News International, the headquarters for the Murdoch media empire, as their arguably Islamaphobic rhetoric can be seen as appealing to such shooters and those who are already so enraged that this can lead to them carrying out other types of hate crimes. It was an evening of poetry, prayer and words, from the Pacific community and from Muslim activists. Sometimes direct action is a vigil, a mural or a silent procession – as we've seen with the residents and community of Grenfell Tower – or simply a space to hear words or be silent and be with others in the face of injustice. However, much of the time, as those facing injustice, when we've used direct action, we're seeking to create, and where necessary, sustain a crisis for our opponents: this direct action allows us to hit our objectives, and our objectives enable us to hit our goals. That is to say that direct action should, more often than not, be facilitating a strategy, and oftentimes direct action misses out on a big opportunity by not being part of a wider sequence, without the follow up to deliver.

STRIKE!

Nick had a wrist propping up his head and appeared uninterested, listening in a way like he'd heard it all before. I told him, half-jokingly, that he doesn't need to worry about me being late to work, as I'm leaving (that day I'd been called in for a disciplinary). That I'm going to camp out at the Occupy Protests we'd both seen on the TV. Nick, who ran the service station, was suddenly slightly more engaged. 'Look, how old are you?' But he dismissed the question as quickly as he said it, 'It doesn't matter. This protest stuff, it doesn't work.' He had this matter-of-fact way of speaking. I moved to interrupt, but decided against it. 'You know I'm from Afghanistan? We're used to protests. You're too young to remember the Iraq demonstration. I went out with the millions of people to stop this Iraq invasion, and you know what that did? Nothing.' Nick, like so many people I've heard since, was clear that protest doesn't work. He had a point, that massive demonstration *didn't* stop the war. However, leaked WikiLeaks cables* show that the anti-war protests, the biggest in human history, combined with the Trident Ploughshare protests and the destruction of military equipment, had indeed created an economic and political crisis, so while the ultimate goal failed, it wasn't all in vain.

---

* 'Cablegate' was the largest ever set of confidential documents to be leaked to the public, by the organisation 'Wikileaks'. Over 250,000 US diplomatic cables revealed a sprawling espionage and spying network seeking to maintain what some refer to as the 'American Empire', including the attempt to subvert and topple Latin American governments and the repeated instances of torture and abuse in Iraq and Afghanistan.

NOTE: Trident Ploughshare is part of the global nuclear disarmament movement, founded in 1998. They aim to disarm the UK Trident nuclear weapons system using non-violent direct action. The Ploughshares movement began in the USA, in 1980, and was made infamous in Britain when four women did £1.5 million damage to an Aerospace Hawk jet, and were acquitted in a Liverpool Crown Court, arguing that they prevented British complicity in the genocide in East Timor.

However, it's true that, with nothing to follow up, no tactical escalation, no sustained crisis, the anti-war marches failed in regards to their primary demand. The US and UK led a devastating 'shock and awe' invasion of Iraq under the false pretences of 'weapons of mass destruction', beginning a war where, according to a comprehensive survey by Opinion Research Business it is estimated that over a million people have died. A war where it has been shown that numerous horrific human rights abuses were committed by British and American soldiers. Fallujah is one such place where the horror of US imperialism – the mass graves, the use of chemical weapons, the shooting dead of groups of unarmed protestors – showed the disdain the Western coalition had for Iraqi life.

When we take direct action, when we agitate, we need to remember that there are hundreds of tactics at an organiser's disposal and many more hundreds yet to be formulated, maybe by you – the issue is that a tactic is only as effective as its application.

TIP

Gene Sharp's list of 198 methods of non-violent direct action, is available online at the Albert Einstein Institution website. A more detailed look at different tactics can be found here: www.beautifulrising.org/type/tactic

---

That is to say that free-floating tactics, such as a mass mobilisation against war, without a long-term strategy behind them, are a sure-fire way to *not* force the hands of power. But, conversely, tactics applied correctly can create a sustained political and/or economic crisis, drastically racking up costs and losses, and are far more likely to win, if winning a goal is the aim.

The Student Non-violent Coordinating Committee (SNCC), a key organisation in the fight for black civil rights in America, used tactics strategically to shift public opinion: they identified white students from the Northern cities as *passive* allies (remember the 'spectrum of allies' from the Organise section?), and used the Freedom Summer, a huge African-American voter registration drive in 1964, to bus them down to the South as volunteers. Witnessing the violence first-hand, these students became *active* allies and decided to take action, writing letters home to their parents, who were often conservative passive opponents. Having read about the killings, arrests and struggles recounted in their children's voices, their parents moved from passive opponents to passive allies. It's important to note how the entire social attitude to civil rights was impacted by this one approach. Nothing was left to chance: every stage was calculated; every direct action was strategic.

Direct action was often the first port of call for me and many of my activist peers; it was the centrepiece of our activism, and everything else seemed to revolve around it. I've been involved in so many direct actions: marches through estates where residents rushed out into the street to join; memorials outside prisons; letter hand-ins at 10 Downing Street over deaths in police custody;

occupations of estates scheduled for demolition; culture jamming – where bus stop advertisements were replaced with information about institutional racism; 'die-ins' over Hostile Environment legislation outside Parliament, closing the main roads; pickets outside worksites where wages had been capped; occupying the central financial district and opening an encampment – there's too many to recall. However, I went along for years thinking that direct action was simply a tool and not educating myself further. It wasn't until a friend and fellow organiser handed me a small book printed by the Solidarity Federation called *Fighting for Ourselves*[1] that I began to question and further understand the history and efficacy of direct action.

The term 'direct action' was first used by the Industrial Workers of the World (IWW), a labour union founded in 1905. It was used to describe an industrial action taking place in Chicago, in 1910, in the form of a strike. Seven years later, during the Seattle General Strike, which the IWW participated heavily in, the city of Seattle shut down for five days, bringing tens of thousands of workers into direct confrontation with the 'captains of industry', the same class of people we face today. Across the

Atlantic at the same time, the Social Democratic Party of Germany was on the cusp of leading a socialist revolution, and further east, a series of industrial actions, mutinies and demonstrations, led by the Soviets (workers' councils) and the Bolshevik party, would topple the Russian empire and install the first socialist state, which, despite its later atrocities under Stalin, initially led a reclamation of life for the everyday worker, legalising LGBT, Jewish and women's rights and inspiring revolutions across the colonised world, throwing the hegemony of global capitalism into direct competition with the rising call for socialism.

Many forms of direct action we still use today: sit-ins, occupations, lock-ons, pickets and strikes, were common during that period, but some actually predate 1910. In the revolutionary era of the eighteenth century, ports were often a hotbed of political activity, where overworked and underpaid sailors spread the news from coast to coast of revolutions toppling the social order, from France to Haiti. As historian Marcus Rediker has related, in an interview with *Radical Philosophy* magazine, in 1768, sailors protesting a wage cut in London went from ship to ship, taking down or 'striking' their sails, and this then went on to become the seafaring origin of the collective action called 'the strike'.[2]

> **TIP**
>
> *Strikes are very important, as they are one of the most powerful weapons in the arsenal of everyday people, yet they are often overlooked as a form of direct action by people new to activism.*

1968 AND ALL THAT

As you might be aware, 1968 was a hell of a year for ordinary people fighting back through direct action. In May, following student occupations in Paris, seven weeks of unrest swept across France, nearly toppling the government. Universities and factories were occupied, and, at its peak, eleven million workers went on strike. Charles De Gaulle, the president at the time, fled to Germany, seeking assurance from the army that they would stand by him. But that wasn't all: that year there was also the Ford Sewing Machinists Strike in Dagenham, the Northern Ireland civil rights struggle, mass movements in Pakistan toppled the president Ayub Khan, there was domestic resistance in the US to the intensifying war in Vietnam, the revolutionary Spring erupted in Prague and the Rodney riots in Jamaica, Olympic athlete Tommie Smith raising the iconic black power fist salute in Mexico from the winner's podium, the racist UK Commonwealth Immigration Act passing after Conservative MP Enoch Powell gave his inflammatory 'Rivers of Blood' speech, the Civil Rights Act of 1968 passed in the US in the wake of Martin Luther King Jnr's assassination, and, on a personal note, my parents ceased to be colonial subjects as Mauritius gained independence.

In respect to creating a crisis, 1968 showed us that there is nothing more powerful than when industrial action and insurrection go hand in hand. There is a hierarchy of impact with tactics, in essence. Where we have achieved our greatest successes, it was down to understanding this hierarchy. Industrial actions, such as strikes, and in particular a General Strike, as witnessed in 1968, have a uniquely powerful ability to put the ruling class on the ropes, by withdrawing the most important factor of production: labour. But mass action like this rarely appears out of thin air, as I've explained: it lives within wider strategies that escalate toward them, which can include deploying lower-impact tactics, such as petitions, first. We live with the successes of these actions every day. It has been a combination of strikes, riots and insurrections that have won many ordinary people their rights over the years.

> **NOTE:** Knowing that we fought for certain rights is empowering, and a powerful argument for getting involved with organising. Rights fought for and won in the UK include the weekend, paid holiday, the eight-hour work day, paid maternity leave, the minimum wage, contracts and protection from discrimination.

CREATIVITY IN PROTEST

My dad is a creative thinker. He was an 'ideas guy' and he had countless get-rich-quick schemes, many of which would probably have caught on too, had he possessed the right social networks. My childhood was filled with stories of his creative attempts to get his many ideas off the ground. He used creativity to fix things in the house too, from stuff in the garden to wobbly stair bannisters. Through him I came to value creativity. I wrote poetry from a young age and never stopped. I'd write short stories and I'd draw all the time. My business partner and old friend Reece is an incredible artist, photographer and thinker. We studied art together at school, quite a few of us did, and we embraced it, but Reece set the pace. We'd spend registrations writing lyrics. Most of my mates and I rapped too: we took the artform seriously. We organised rap 'clashes', which take heritage from Jamaican sound clashing, between school members but also between schools, which sometimes attracted a 100-person-strong audience. All these creative abilities are skills that I've found to be transferable to the art of protest. Whether it's subtle humorous creativity, such as the huge crowds who jangled their keys during the Czech revolution in 1989, indicating it was time for Russian influence to go home, or whether it's the film, music and artwork that coloured Britain's longest industrial dispute, the miners' strike – protest should *always* be creative.

In 2017, a mind-blowing ten-part seventeen-hour docu-series called *The Vietnam War*, directed by Ken Burns, premiered on American television channel PBS. One of the most harrowing moments in the documentary are the clips about the My Lai

Massacre, taken from a 1969 interview between CBS reporter Mike Wallace and soldier Paul Meadlo. Wallace asks Meadlo about his role and who he killed. 'Men, women and children?' Wallace asks. 'Men, women and children,' Meadlo responded. 'And babies?' There's a pause before Meadlo repeats, 'and babies'. It was a soul-searching moment for American society at the time. The Art Workers' Coalition, a group of New York City artists, then reclaimed those four words, turning it into an anti-war poster that became iconic and especially powerful.

Equally, in her book *Memes to Movements*,[3] technologist and writer An Xiao Mina explains how ACT UP, an international movement to end the AIDS pandemic in the 1980s, used the pink triangle, which the Nazis had used to mark out queer people in concentration camps, who were often subjected to the worst abuse. ACT UP took the triangle, turned it upside down, and made it their logo. Later, queer activists would develop a more positive and affirming symbol – the rainbow flag – and later still, racialised and trans activists would add the colours brown and blue to represent the struggle of racialised queer people and trans people.

The modern meme, however, is the ultimate form of reclamation: it is peak remix culture. Tumblr Librarian Amanda Brennan simply defines memes as 'pieces of content that travel from person to person and change along the way'. A meme, be it a cat or person, can be remixed and imbued with culture, with story and meaning, which is what allows it to travel and catch so fast. Xiao Mina calls memes the 'street art of the social web', and explains how, in relation to protest, they help create the 'digital plaza', which mirrors the physical plazas of places such as Tiananmen or Tahrir Square. The hundreds of memes that are currently circulating social media in 2020, mocking the British government's 'Stay Alert' messaging during the Coronavirus Pandemic, for example, are an easy and direct challenge to the government narrative. Sharing a meme like this is a form of protest, and it is often many people's first form of protest. Xiao Mina's book shows the vital importance of thinking through the visual culture that we imbue our organisations with, and how activist movements were actually some of the first places to really explode open remix culture, through badges, pins and posters. Memes can help you harness the creative and political power of the imagination, and rebuild narratives online.

The combination of creative outlets and direct action allows protest to be not just a confrontation with police, but a powerful, memorable and inspiring moment. I've seen this in other parts of the world, such as Latin America, where protesters often use body paint, and also in the protest music from India and Pakistan. Witnessing all this made many of us realise that we're way behind the curve when it comes to creativity in Britain. So, with BLMUK, we made it a staple of how we protest to never have print-out placards. Instead, public placard-making sessions, with heaps of paints, pens and materials, were a fundamental part of the work. We also got super creative through the repeated use of culture jamming, a tactic used by anti-consumerist movements to disrupt and subvert media, installing 'subvertisements' at bus stops around the country, for example, formatted as UK Home Office announcements, alerting the public to the statistics we think they need to know, but also to the UFFC (United Friends & Family Campaign) annual procession for people who have died in state custody.

Art, music and creativity will always be at the heart of the revolutionary struggle, as Claudia Jones, a pioneering journalist and political activist, and mother of the Notting Hill Carnival, once said, 'a people's art is the genesis of their freedom'.

NO JUSTICE, NO PEACE

Gloria offered me some snacks and wine, leftovers from a party. She was well, and in good spirits, but her health condition had been giving her grief. Sitting at the desk, Pat said she just needed to take her foot off the gas. It was true, to be honest: Gloria is one of the most tireless campaigners I know. I'd been aware of her and JENGbA's (Joint Enterprise Not Guilty by Association) work for some years now. For me, they're one of the most important organisations in the country. JENGbA is a group of mostly mothers and family members of people wrongly imprisoned under the Joint Enterprise legal doctrine, a 300-year-old law, which allows a jury to convict people on the vague fringes of a crime on the same charge as those who committed it. Put plainly, simply living in the vicinity, being in close proximity or just knowing someone involved in the crime can be used to justify complicity and can result in mandatory life sentences. No assistance, no encouragement, no foresight, no real connection to a death is necessarily needed. The scale of injustice is unfathomable, and also difficult to quantify as British courts don't record when someone is sentenced through Joint Enterprise doctrine, the only way to estimate is by looking at instances of group murder convictions, and looking further through court transcripts. By this estimate JENGbA anticipate that there are thousands of people locked up because of it, and it is part of why Britain has the highest proportion of mandatory lifers in Western Europe.

UK rapper Potter Payper details how joint enterprise works in his song 'Carpe Diem'. Having personally lost many friends to charges of murder, he sees it as a way for the government and police to put as many people behind bars as possible. In one case in Manchester back in 2016, eleven people were convicted, and given mandatory life sentences, for a murder committed by one person. Currently, black people are serving prison time under the Joint Enterprise Doctrine at eleven times the rate of the rest of the population because of the gross association of blackness and criminality. As the aunt of one of those convicted in Manchester said: 'They saw black boys from Moss Side, they heard "gangs", and that was it.' And Gloria explained to me how most people who are sentenced under joint enterprise had no idea what was taking place, and then they were suddenly sentenced for something they didn't do.

It was maybe my third or fourth time at their small office at the bottom of a tower block on an estate in West London, so I felt comfortable moving around the cabinets and chairs. I was there for a slightly unconventional reason: filming for a music video. The filing cabinet, standing about 5ft high, is a site of mass injustice. Within it are several hundred files, each file a person in prison, charged under Joint Enterprise. I've seen Gloria talk about the issue in public on numerous occasions, and chaired her on more than one of them. She is a walking cabinet of information herself and can paint a picture, clear as day, of how the criminal justice system is often rigged to punish the poor.

LAW AND STRATEGY

'Laws aren't unchangeable, they simply represent the views of those in power at this point in time': these words are taken from the iconic direct-action group Sisters Uncut, in their online guide to taking direct action. Sisters Uncut have used creative non-violent direct action in ways that deserve careful study, and have kept the brutal cuts to domestic violence services high up on the political agenda. Their demand is urgent: end the austerity cuts to domestic violence services. They organise across London and in several cities across the country. What I take from their words above is that it is incumbent upon us as activists to recognise that the law, for the most part, is not working for working-class people, that it has zero legitimacy. A large proportion of us connected intimately to the struggles of injustice will know this from how our friends, family and wider communities have been abused by the criminal justice system. Wretch 32's song 'Liberation' addresses the fight for freedom. There are many living examples around the world today that show us certain people may feel it is necessary to engage in civil disobedience. However, a word of caution, as someone who has got to know the criminal justice system intimately: as much as possible we should avoid our activists, organisers, members and organisations being unnecessarily arrested and dragged through that system.

However, it is undeniable that sometimes arrests are the most powerful direct action to advance the strategy. We've seen this with the brave and powerful actions of the 'Stansted 15' – fifteen non-violent activists who blocked an airport runway in order to stop a chartered deportation flight, and to raise awareness of the government's Hostile Environment policy. Due to their actions, eleven people are still in the UK today, four have been referred as victims of human trafficking, and one person has been granted leave to remain. More often, though, arrests are an undesirable outcome, which becomes a huge drain on organisational resources.

TIP

If you or your fellow members are engaging in civil disobedience, then it is imperative that you use legal briefings for participants, legal observation for the duration of the action, have 'bust cards' – printed with some of your rights and emergency contact numbers – to distribute to protestors, and you should have sympathetic law practices on call. Organisations such as the Network for Police Monitoring and the Green and Black Cross websites have a lot of resources. Also, if you do get arrested for civil disobedience (or anything, for that matter), you are allowed to offer 'no comment' and, from my personal experience, I'd advise you to never take a duty solicitor. Green and Black Cross have lots of information on which legal firms are best placed to take up political cases, and how to access legal aid.

THE CRIME OF BEING BLACK

The sun was out and I felt it was going to be a good day. I made a pit stop at a local newsagents on the way to a friend's birthday drinks in a park not too far away. Inside I couldn't find the drink I was after, so I left, acknowledging the shopkeeper on my way out with a nod – a necessary ritual that communicates so much, and in this instance that I hadn't stolen anything. I was almost to the door and then, as with so many times before: 'Hey, you'. For my own dignity, I couldn't cooperate in that moment, and nor could I cooperate all the other times I had been mis-branded a thief by a shopkeeper who has racially profiled me. He insists I've stolen something. I tell him he's made a mistake, but this moment hits too close to the bone, and in an instant I've regressed into the eleven-year-old me who was banned from the school corner store due to a false allegation. However, I make it clear to him that I am leaving. He leaves the shop too, takes his phone out and starts following and filming me. Before I know it, we are both on the pavement scuffling. Out of nowhere a person I presume is a student from the local university is pinning my legs down, but a black man with his kids in tow pulls both of them off me. Somehow we all end up back at the original corner shop, where he has locked the door, and we are going blow for blow. I fall over a stand and the impact of hitting the ground knocks me out. Twenty seconds later I come to with blood oozing down my ear from where he's sunk in his teeth. He was crazed, his hands locked around my neck. I go to shout, but only a tiny high-pitched squeak escapes. I suddenly realise how fragile life is – a minute more and I could have been gone. An older black lady starts screaming nearby, a guardian angel maybe: 'You're gonna kill him!' The shopkeeper looks away, I pull his arms away, get up, and ask: 'What are you, the police!?' His final words? 'When you're here, yes, I am.'

In his song 'XXX', rapper Kendrick Lamar talks about how America creates an image of violence in relation to the black man, and the black community, but that this is a mirror image of America itself, and the violence it has wrought on these communities. The same is historically true of Britain (and remains so), the finer details of which, our American cousins learnt from and embraced. But this violent image is one that we work hard to recreate ourselves from youth: it's a self-fulfilling prophecy, a projection that lives on in the psyche; to be the hardest and most ruthless is an image we strive for as working-class racialised men. This very same super strong, super violent image is also one that figures of authority routinely maintain against racialised people of whatever gender. It's why four officers were 'needed' to question Cynthia Jarrett, aged 49, who died of heart failure in North London. Or why three deportation officers, a 4ft restraint belt, handcuffs and 13ft of tape were used to detain Joy Gardner, until she stopped breathing and later died. This almost always unwarranted image marks us out for violence and criminalisation. Sometimes this violence ruptures at the surface, as with my story above; sometimes it shows itself in the rates of school exclusions, incarcerations and deportations. State violence is how society works: it's the lubricant, as Kendrick notes in the same song.

For all of these reasons and more, conversations around violence still really baffle me. Depending on which section of society you live in, violence is either ordinary or extraordinary. Violence is how the system expresses itself to us and how we then express it to each other. I've witnessed poverty and austerity kill my neighbours slowly.

I've experienced being taken to the Old Bailey by the state on claims of violent disorder. At various points in my life I've had knives, coshes, bats, bricks and guns pulled on me. I've watched a young person bleed to death in my arms through avoidable youth violence. Violence is often a hallmark of life for marginalised communities; every disparity in educational attainment, in criminal sentencing, in wages, is a structural violence that cashes out in lower life expectancy, higher suicide rates and an overall lower quality of life in our communities. Society has a constant backdrop of violence, and it's from this backdrop that rebellion often emerges. To my mind, there is no moral ground lost in the mass of people making it plainly clear that in political struggle to paraphrase abolitionist Frederick Douglas slightly, sometimes you cannot have the rain without thunder and lightning, or the ocean without the roar of its many waters. If we do choose thunder and lightning, though, it should be because it is tactically appropriate, and now or in the future, those moments that call for the roar of the ocean will surely occur.

The Boston Tea Party, which took place in 1773, is on nearly every school syllabus in America. It's the story of how the American revolution began, a story of how American colonists, angry over Britain's decision to increase tax prices on tea, boarded three ships loaded with said British tea – which the British had, arguably, looted from China – and spent four hours looting in turn, pouring over 90,000 pounds of tea into the Boston Harbour. Some of the group allegedly dressed as Native Americans, so that they had a scapegoat. Today, these men, who destroyed millions of pounds' worth of property, all in the name of tea, are lauded as heroes and patriots. One of them is revered as a founding father of the USA.

Yet, at the time of writing this book, millions of people around the world have taken to the streets around the world in the George Floyd Uprising, to protest the routine institutional murder of black and brown people – in some cases setting on fire police stations, youth prisons and smashing some shop fronts along the way – and all these people are being demonised for their actions. We forget the lineage of history, and often wear rose-tinted glasses when the facts of the matter are the same. America, much like Britain, was founded upon acts of vandalism, violence and property destruction, but it's who's doing that destruction that ultimately determines how it will be seen, whether it will be demonised or revered.

Before Malcolm X brought the phrase into popular consciousness, Frantz Fanon, the political philosopher, would address a conference in Accra, Ghana, in 1960 and speak of the 'diverse, repeated, cumulative violence' colonised people face, and the need to end colonialism 'by any means necessary'. So often this is painted as a justification for damage and violence; however, this interpretation neglects the nuances and also the history of those words. There has been an unbroken line of violence perpetrated by the ruling class for four centuries: it is how Britain built its empire, well before it became Great Britain: it is in this nation's DNA. It still is today. At the time of writing, statistics have revealed that racialised communities in Britain are dying at a heavily disproportionate rate to their white counterparts from the Covid-19 Pandemic, as a result of *repeated, cumulative racist inequalities* in access to quality healthcare, safe work and safe housing. Precisely because we are racialised, we are more likely to die. This example of the violence of racism, in access to health, in education, in employment, is a trace of history, it is a violence that goes right back to colonisation. The fact remains that this is a question of strategy, not morality: it is strategic to bear arms as a means of defence, and as a means of saving lives. As historian Robin D. G. Kelley wrote when reviewing Akinyele Omowale Umoja's *We Will Shoot Back: Armed Resistance in the Mississippi Freedom Movement*,[4] 'armed self-defence actually saved lives, reduced terrorist attacks on African American communities, and laid the foundation for unparalleled community solidarity.'

People often conveniently forget that violence was the equally important counterpart to the civil disobedience of the US Civil Rights struggle, as the journalist Ta-Nehisi Coates writes on the matter: 'the Civil Rights Bill of 1964 is inseparable from the threat of riots. The housing bill of 1968 – the most proactive civil-rights legislation on the books – is a direct response to the riots that swept American cities after King was killed. Violence, lingering on the outside, often backed nonviolence during the civil-rights movement.'[5] Similarly, people are far too quick to champion Gandhi as the prime mover of Indian independence, and slow to remember the necessarily violent tactics of people like Bhagat

Singh, or forget to recall that apartheid would not have ended without armed insurgency – after non-violence failed.

I'm also extremely aware of the trauma it inflicts on its survivors, as well as on its perpetrators, and how people can be both at the same time because of the ubiquity of violence. I believe that, where possible, we can and should avoid unnecessary trauma, but I also believe that, in order to wise up to the gravity of the situation we find ourselves in, we must be as strategic as possible, and this means 'no cards should be off the table', that there are times when violence may well be politically expedient. Those times are far from the political moment we find ourselves in, in Britain, but we can't rule out the possibility that it's a context we may find ourselves in as the status quo unwinds. While imprisoned by fascist leader Mussolini, Antonio Gramsci wrote a theory of two battlefronts: the War of Position and the War of Manoeuvre. The War of Position is where we conduct most of our political struggle, across the institutions of civil society, building power and entrenching the argument that the ideological hegemony of the ruling class is illegitimate. Whereas the War of Manoeuvre is the direct confrontation with the ruling class, and it is a near inevitable situation, simply because history has shown that, time and again, the ruling class will resort to their monopoly over violence.

CHAPTER 8

GET TEACHING

We put away our smokes and began to cut across the stone paths toward the interviewee's home. The open-plan living space meant I could see through two rooms back towards the kitchen, where somebody was coming over with tea. It was always like this, as tea was the ritual that made talking possible. Oons and I had a couple of exchanges, making sure we were on the same page, and then I opened up the monopod, fixed the lens on, found a comfortable position, and began working through the settings. I'd known Oons for quite a few years now – she's an incredible documentarian and got me started on film-making – and by then things felt intuitive between us. The whole family had come for the interview, little ones and elders, and it was one of the best interviews we caught whilst in Eastern Turkey.

We were not far from the Syrian border, in a village where my friend, who was with us to vouch and translate, had recommended we come to meet returned, injured fighters from Rojava. It was through these fighters and other interviewees that we would build a more complete picture of the revolution taking place. One of the younger women made a dig at the father, about him knowing his place now that women are front and centre in the revolutionary struggle. The mother laughed and the father made a joke back. Oons smiled and asked if someone could explain the political philosophy she was hinting at a bit further. One of the young men talked us through this educational element of the political movement: 'liberation is not possible without women's liberation'.

I was fortunate enough, a couple years later, to be invited to join an education session with a visiting educator of a political movement in Rojava. We spent a day discussing the history, strategy and successes of this hugely influential political movement, whose embrace of libertarian socialism and consequent revolution in Rojava is inspiring activists across the globe. What stood out to me then, as it had those years before in the interview I filmed with Oons, was that the long-standing tradition of collective political education has been intrinsic to their freedom struggle for decades. The Kurdish education programme often consists of military strategy, but also spiritual tradition (hakitat), scientific discipline and feminism (jineology). The educator told us how a small group of students, the founding members of the modern struggle, went on to cultivate a movement of over ten million members, including armed regiments, numerous schools of political and military learning, and international delegations. What was cherished then in the beginning, as it is now, was the need to both 'teach in' *and* 'teach out', in a structured and consistent way.

The success of their education programme can be measured in the shifting dynamics of social attitudes and the changing face of political leadership. From my experiences with this political movement in Rojava, I took forward the importance of political education as an avenue for transformation both within our political organisations, but also within wider society. However we choose to build in a programme of political education, whichever format(s) we do it in, it should always be internal *and* external, symbiotic *and* dynamic, in that both processes inform each other: 'teach in' and 'teach out'.

In a 2008 interview with the *Guardian*, legendary dub poet Linton Kwesi Johnson discusses how he first met Altheia Jones-Le Cointe, the leader of the British Black Panther movement, saying she was, 'perhaps the most remarkable woman I've ever met.' Jones-LeCointe was a 'Panther Teacher' and spoke regularly at schools, teaching classes of community education in anti-colonialism and more. He points to this as 'where [he] got his real education'. Furthermore, that 'I was able to locate myself in the world and to understand myself more fully. Who I am, where I'm coming from and why I am where I am now. A whole new world opened itself to me and I started reading all kinds of stuff. It was the formative period of my life.'[6]

Fewer things create more of a crisis for the rich than when a methodical approach to insurgent political education becomes popular, countering the mainstream and driving a wedge between the people and the political establishment. A political education that enables the majority of us to read the world for what it is, and call bullshit. If most of us had access to this type of genuine political education, if we had the language to name what we've always felt and the permission to act, then the system would be on its knees by the weekend. However, political education has fallen out of vogue in many activist groups, and the Black Panther P. E. (political education) classes, which once awoke a slumbering giant within our communities, seem to have become something of the past.

Before going any further, I think it's important to note that political education, since it is not doing the work of mainstream education, does not need to look or feel like mainstream education. The work of agitating through political education should not be a recreation of school. It should and can use all the tools available: memes, games, video tutorials, digital resources, print materials, and this list is nowhere near exhaustive. It's one of the most exciting challenges for organisers: how do we raise political consciousness (our own and others) in the era of DIY media? 'Get teaching' could well be a mantra – it's about agitating ourselves and our wider communities with radical education, where, as Angela Davis says, 'radical simply means grasping things at the root', because when our organisations and their wider communities can read the world, there is no task more urgent than to change it. Like Kwesi Johnson, I was fortunate to get a good chunk of my political education in the black radical tradition. It meant that I was exposed to rich ideologies, such as black feminist socialist thinking, alive with not just theory but story, poetry, music. This education didn't just elevate my politics but also my sense of self, place and my commitment to unlearn the prejudices I've absorbed throughout my life. The groups in this tradition that I organised with and around valued political education highly, and it was a cornerstone of our work. Whether through community workshops, or film screenings, we saw that collective consciousness raising, inviting people to value their own knowledge, was a primary way of building political struggle.

Broadly speaking, social movements and activists too often substitute political education for workshops and training, offering individualised skill sets: power and privilege, non-violent direct action, conflict resolution, anti-racism, inclusion and unconscious bias. These skills are all very important elements of doing great activism, but cannot substitute for insurgent political education. The primary role of the political education I'm speaking about is to invoke class, race and gender consciousness. Invocation is done with 'revolutionary theory'.

In the instance of the British Black Panther party under Jones-LeCointe, this was theory rooted in the black, feminist, revolutionary socialist tradition. It's something that cannot happen as most things do – in a two-day workshop, say.

What often happens for people newly into activism is that this learning happens outside of organisations, and largely online. Whilst there's certainly nothing wrong with learning online, learning with others, being encouraged to learn through our own experiences, being taught by experienced, participatory educators as part of an organisational programme, is incomparable. Anti-colonial leader Amilcar Cabral, who helped organise one of the most complete revolutionary defeats of a coloniser on the African continent, spoke of how his party disseminated political education in waves. First, the 'militants from the towns were the first to come to receive political instruction and to be trained in how to mobilise our people for the struggle'. Then, he recounts, 'comrades from the city came, peasants and youths – even bringing their entire families – who had been mobilised by Party members. During that period, they went through an intensive education programme.'[*][7]

But, the past is not always a place from which we have advanced; sometimes the past is where we need to advance towards. I often wonder what would an approach to political education in this vein look like today?

---

[*] Amílcar Cabral was born in Guinea-Bissau in 1924. He was an important thinker and political organiser, significant in pushing for the absolute independence of Portuguese colonies during the 1950s. In 1956 he founded PAIGC (Partido Africano para a Independência da Guiné).

WHAT are the lessons we can take from political education programmes of the past?

HOW would we use the assortment of new media available to us?

HOW can we use archives, or whatever is closest to you, as a way of enriching teaching?

Political education could potentially look like an educational programme offered both internally and externally, including:

LOOKING: at our cultures of resistance in the past through exploring the archives, be it the thinking, strategies or the action.

MAKING: zines, memes, digital resources, online courses, posters, archives.

DOING: historical tours or walks.

BUILDING: a physical learning establishment that services our movement internally and the local communities we exist within.

> **OFFERING:** low cost or free skills and training, especially for those who have difficulty in accessing them, such as migrants and asylum seekers.

Whatever avenue we pursue, our groups should have a unique approach to teaching, our members should be getting educated, and, most importantly, we should become *community* educators, learning from and within our communities.

CRITICAL PEDAGOGY

Critical pedagogy is an indispensable concept when thinking about what political education is trying to do. If pedagogy is simply an approach to education and teaching, then critical pedagogy is an approach that helps people assess, question and challenge their circumstances, reaching what Paolo Freire calls 'critical consciousness' – the ability to engage with political and social contradictions, and change them. Critical pedagogy also suggests that people already have the majority of the tools at their disposal to begin to read the world, in the form of our experiences.

Across 2019/2020, I worked on a film project called *Our Homes*, where we worked with residents in my local area to use film to research the root causes of the broken housing system, and then explore how to take action against it. The educational method we used, Participatory Action Research, uses film-making and community research as a critical pedagogy, and was an incredibly powerful way to learn, research and gain insights together and from each other. Through methods like this, people can really begin to analyse their circumstances. As important as being able to analyse, however, is being able to raise revolutionary thinking, and a vision of where we might go from here. 'Nobody has yet made a successful revolution without a *revolutionary theory*' – Amílcar Cabral's wisdom here is a reiteration of what Vladimir Lenin had understood many decades before: 'without revolutionary theory, there can be no revolutionary movement. This idea cannot be insisted upon too strongly'. Some things simply need to be taught, and as Lenin suggested in the same pamphlet, 'What is to be Done: The Burning Questions of Our Movement', they should also be taught with plenty of opportunity to be interrogated and criticised. The revolutionary thinking of Angela Davis, of Gloria Anzaldua, of Walter Rodney, of

Claudia Jones, of Tithi Bhattacharya, of Silvia Federici, of Steve Biko and so many more have much to offer us when it comes to reading the world, and understanding the violent grip of the system. The great shame is that much theorising is tough to read, and often difficult for your average reader to get into. So, then, the task is to get into it together, to form reading groups, to dig out the eureka! moments, and use it for wider political education. Bringing our wider communities into revolutionary thinking is an attitude of solidarity, it's an invitation into a shared journey, as we're all always learning.

There's a story in *Heart of the Race*, where a woman talks about the first time she met Claudia Jones, which I think is worth reproducing in full:

> *'I was in the launderette and she must have noticed me sitting there alone, depressed and on the verge of tears. She had been reading, and she put her book to one side, and came over to talk to me. I told her about the problems I was having at the time with accommodation – I was living with my three very young children in one room on hardly any money . . . I remember her telling me that all Black people throughout the world were going*

through the same kind of experiences. Then she helped
me claim social security.

Claudia was always like that. She could talk to you in
political terms, and explain things very clearly, but she
was also there with the practical help, too. She was a
wealth of knowledge, and she explained a lot of political
matters to me. She stopped me from going around
thinking that what was happening to me here was my
fault. This really encouraged me to do some thinking
and some reading for myself . . . I now started to read
some serious books. Claudia even gave me a booklist!
This was the beginning of my involvement in politics.[8]

Offering political perspective is an act of solidarity, a
natural extension of a gift that someone once gifted
us in turn. That is the origin of the phrase 'each one,
teach one', and it came from the plantations. When
a freed enslaved person was able to access further
education, it was incumbent upon them to pass on that
gift, the gift of education, and in this case it's political
education. I have come across some phenomenal
examples of critical pedagogy in practice, below are a
couple, but there are hundreds more, all of which can
help model a programme of political education that
sits within your political organisation.

CONSENTED: ran for two years, printed a regular magazine and hosted public events. Through the print magazine, the youth edited editions, the summer schools, and workshops, it was about lifting our ability to read the world, and seeing our stories on the page. They empowered young people into political agency, and some of them continue to do incredible activism and political work.

VOICES THAT SHAKE!: now ten years old, 'reclaims art as a tool for societal change, personal well-being and transformational learning' and has engaged hundreds of young people through workshops and skill-shares. Through these, young people are introduced into campaigning and encouraged to interrogate their circumstances and society. Many alumni have gone on to set up their own organisations.

EACH ONE, TEACH ONE

I'm part of a group called APAC (A People's Art Collective). We borrowed the words from Claudia Jones, who talked about art as essential to freedom fighting. To me, this also means that the road towards freedom begins with culture, and not just any culture, but a people's culture. A people's culture will be a people's political education, whether we like it or not.

Popular culture has provided me with a first-class political education, in both the right and wrong ways. As explained in the Educate section, in popular culture you'll find traces of mainstream hegemony, and you'll also find instances of counter-hegemony. You'll often find both of these in the most iconic artists of their times, be it Beyoncé or David Bowie. If we believe that it is the mass of people who will throw off the yoke of imperialist, capitalist, white-supremacist patriarchy, then we meet people where we are, in culture. Activists and activist groups should be engaging with popular culture with their political education, both by using it and by adding to it. Can we teach anti-imperialism through Palestinian rap? Can we unpack masculinity through Lauryn Hill's, or Jay Z's body of work? Can we explore class struggle through Ken Loach's films? Can we maybe interpret the creativity of revolt through Álex Pina's television series *Money Heist*?

The news services also form a big part of main-stream culture, and it's another space of potential interruption and for providing political education. The Black Panther newspaper remains one of the most iconic and powerful tools of agitation employed by the party, just as the *Workers Dreadnought*, which Sylvia Pankhurst and the East London Federation of Suffragettes published, was an invaluable resource in community education and upliftment. These educational institutions became part of everyday culture. Despite all that's been said about the Occupy movement, for and against, the fact was, as with most political projects, it was learning as it went along, but the two most iconic institutions that Occupy London set up were *The Occupied Times of London*, and Tent City University, and these were set up within two weeks of the occupation. *The Occupied Times* was a truly incredible newspaper, which lived on for six years after the encampment was evicted, and Tent City University was ground-breaking. A 'Campus under Canvas', as the *Independent* put it, we had guest speakers from many fields, all providing lectures on all things economic. These institutions provided the beating heart of the encampment, circulating around the few hundred people and wider communities, and lifting our collective consciousness.

It all comes back to 'each one, teach one' – the ethos of agitating through a methodical approach to political education, enriched by revolutionary thinking; it's the work of freeing our minds from the muck of imperialist, capitalist, white-supremacist patriarchy. By teaching in and teaching out, and tapping into popular culture, we can create a popular spirit of political struggle. A struggle filled with visionary ideas of exactly what can come next, exactly what kinds of strategies are applicable to this moment, and the skills to read the world and fight back against the unending attack on our daily lives.

CHAPTER 9

GET FREE

FORWARD IN FEMINISM

In 1978, political theorist and activist Zillah Eisenstein published an anthology entitled *Capitalist Patriarchy and the Case for Socialist Feminism*. In it was one of the cornerstones of Black Feminism, the Combahee River Collective Statement. This statement was drafted by Barbara Smith, Demita Frazier and Beverley Smith, and all three came to the collective from a rich history of fighting for freedom, and exploring and being enriched by various ideological positions. Demita Frazier was part of the Chicago chapter of the Black Panther Party, organised with the Young Socialist Alliance and was part of the Jane Collective, helping women access safe abortions. Barbara Smith was part of Students for a Democratic Society, participated in the '68 Columbia University strike action and is often credited with founding Black Women's Studies. Beverley Smith (no relation), meanwhile, was active in the Congress on Racial Equality, where she met organising giant Fannie Lou Hamer and became involved in the Freedom Schools.

It is these three and the wider group's vast political experiences that injected socialist, internationalist and black feminist meaning into that ground-breaking document. It goes without saying that you should go and read the statement. But here's an excerpt:

> 'We realize that the liberation of all oppressed peoples necessitates the destruction of the political-economic systems of capitalism and imperialism as well as patriarchy. We are socialists because we believe that work must be organized for the collective benefit of those who do the work and create the products, and not for the profit of the bosses. Material resources must be equally distributed among those who create these resources. We are not convinced, however, that a socialist revolution that is not also a feminist and anti-racist revolution will guarantee our liberation.'[9]

To the Combahee River Collective, subscribing to the politics of black feminist socialism was not the solution, though. The solution was to then 'make a clear leap into revolutionary action'.[10] Being political in service to doing politics. In doing politics, we make these critically important beliefs no longer niche, but mainstream. As previous chapters have shown, we need to get organised, get strategic and get our hands on power to do that.

The vision that the black-feminist-socialist political programme can offer us is a new, free society. One where racism, sexism, hetero-sexism, transphobia, ableism and class no longer exist. One where prisons, police and borders are obsolete and the humanising work of abolitionist feminism guides how we deal with harm and accountability. One where the necessity of bosses and landlords no longer exists. One where workers own the means of production, and localised economies work hand in hand with nature. One where we can finally have time, energy and access to happiness, which can be enjoyed with our family, friends, loved ones and communities.

In our fight for change, it is incumbent upon us to become visionary, as Robin D. G. Kelley instructs us, to hone in on our freedom dreams. Every brilliant vision we can call upon is not handed down from the mountains by God but is the work of people like you and me, people in our communities, coming together and imagining a better life. The world provides us with no shortage of horrific visions, but it also offers us occasional joys, momentary senses of equality and fairness that are affirmative glimpses of what we can dream for. We need to come together to really imagine and realise a vision of the future. In doing this, we are also summoned to engage the visionary traditions of the past, be it revolutionary socialism or black feminism. We need to put ourselves into the shoes of our heroes, to imbibe the strategic cunning of Nanny of the Maroons* to channel the immovable voice of revolutionary socialist Rosa Luxemburg. Our heroes developed spectacular visions of the free world we fight for, and we'd do well to study their merits and apply them to the struggle as it stands today.

SOLIDARITY IS OUR SUPERPOWER

I struggle to find the words to describe the calamities that the global poor are facing. The violence meted out moment to moment is more grotesque than most visions of hell we might summon: the bombs and war, the ruthless search for profit at any cost, the criminalisation of migration that transforms deserts and seas into mass graves for so-called

---

* Nanny was a military, religious and political leader of the Blue Mountain Maroon community in Jamaica in the late seventeenth and early eighteenth century. She led the large community towards peace and prosperity, but also successfully in war against the British imperialists.

'illegals'. From strip searches in the 'hood to mountaintops being blown off to access precious minerals, we are witnessing new and extreme forms of degradation. The centre truly cannot hold. We feel it, we see it, we watch as the most questionable and immoral humans parade as leaders of the 'free world', governing arsenals capable of destroying the globe several times over, while capitalist economies destroy our world only slightly more slowly – testing the very possibility of future life on earth.

What I can say to you, the reader, with complete certainty, is that if we continue to live under this system, where the ruling classes show complete disregard for the lives of working people and the natural environment, then in the space of just one lifetime human society will become completely unrecognisable, hellish in new and unthinkable ways. Runaway climate change will lead to devastation not just in the magnitude and frequency of extreme weather events, but in relation to how nation-states choose to contain and protect their economies. Food insecurity, wars, extreme weather and economic crises will force hundreds of millions to leave their homes, and if the racist, xenophobic beast that we call national citizenship remains, then borders will become even greater sites of mass murder. Food, water, air and movement: many of us take these things for granted. But if we stay on our current path, it is not clear we will be able to for much longer.

This apocalyptic vision of the future is only the extension of the histories that brought us to this point: imperialism, colonialism and capitalism have been the story of the modern world. As many colonised peoples have expressed, there is an unbroken line of violence from then to now, and so it has been the end of the world for four hundred years. As pressing as the situation feels now, this fight is a long one, and it demands of us both patience *and* pace. We cannot rush the work of political change. What we know is that, in the face of such a backward, violent and morally bankrupt economic and social system, only a complete transformation will suffice.

'I Am A Revolutionary': was the call and response of slain Black Panther Party member Fred Hampton whenever a crowd was gathered. To Hampton, it was important that we become brave, that we accept our roles as agents of change, that we all become revolutionary. Revolutionaries are clichéd figures, seen as extremist and outdated, but the revolutionary person Hampton spoke of was in fact our neighbour, our work colleague, our aunty, and even our supposed enemy – all potential comrades. Revolutionaries have day jobs and care responsibilities, but they approach the world with the knowledge that we need to abolish the system, not just tweak it. In history we see time and again that it is ordinary working people who transform not only their circumstances but the fate of the world when they gather together with the mass of oppressed and exploited people around them.

Hampton understood that we needed to be out in our surroundings, organising in the daily struggle, inspiring others into action. Hampton worked on several community service programmes, including free breakfast for school kids and a free medical clinic, but his work on movement building is what cemented him in history. Hampton, and the Chicago Black Panthers Chapter, used solidarity as the glue to bind together as wide a coalition of resistance as possible, he believed it was central to the radial humanism that he and the Panthers espoused to help communities empathise with one another, and overcome division. The result was the

Rainbow Coalition, which included the National Young Lords, the Young Patriots Organisation, the Students for a Democratic Society, the Blackstone Rangers, the American Indian Movement, the Red Guard, the Brown Berets and the Poor People's Coalition: everyone committed to radical change and transformation. In the Rainbow Coalition lay the seeds of an idea, one which is capable of toppling empires: the people united can never be defeated. Hampton's spirit is what we need to summon today. The spirit of building people power, and the spirit of revolution.

Political activism has perhaps never been more important. The good news is that we can win. The even better news is that this is not a game of chance, but the work of head and heart and science. If we activate our collective power by utilising the many lessons available to us, lessons expressed in this book and beyond, then we will win. If you take up the struggle, we will win.

Whoever you are, wherever you are, whatever your circumstances, whether in the jailhouse, the nursing ward, in college or in limbo, you have what it takes to make change around you. You don't need a formal education in politics or philosophy. In fact, it's people like you and me, who might not have had that formal education, who have been the people who have made enormous political change over the centuries. Don't wait for someone else to do it, don't count on our political leaders – get educated, get organised, get active and get free.

acknowledgements

I acknowledge and am grateful for many things in relation to this book.

For the often thankless work, care and support, visible and invisible, which reproduces all activism, and makes all revolutionary work possible: those who clean the community centres, who cook, who transport, who share a variety of care responsibilities, who listen and advise, who translate and who build accessible, inclusive structures.

For the revolutionary torchbearers who lit the pathway to this moment. Those who in purges and pogroms have sheltered the struggle for freedom and maintained visions of a freer world. Those activists who when police knocked on their doors, and when governments outlawed their pamphlets, continued to whisper stories of revolt to their children, to sing songs of freedom with their peers, and who refused to accept injustice in its many forms. If not for them, we might live in a much darker world.

For the freedom fighters I've met across the world, in refugee camps on the Syrian border, in burger joints in Lahore. Those who fight the ruling elite where they are, to make real the possibility of freedom everywhere, beyond borders. The internationalist spirit of these freedom fighters has left an indelible impression on my beliefs, and it lives in and through the pages of this book.

For the ideas and images of the documentarians, novelists, theorists, musicians, dancers, artists and poets, whose creative works have inspired my thinking, and lifted my heart. There are truly too many to name, but many will be found amidst the book and in the Everyday Resources section.

For my parents, grandparents and ancestors, who refused the hand they were dealt, and took all the small steps which made it possible for me to have the means to learn, write and speak back. For my Pops, you instilled a sense of dignity, showed me your records, your little bookshelf and gave me some respite from the one-way thinking of school and church. For my sisters, as ready to cuss me out as you are to encourage me to be my best self, this is precisely why I love you. For Ma, it's from you I get my nerve, that which I treasure most.

For all those whom I've organised with, demonstrated with, trained with, cried with, eaten with, laughed with, raged with, learnt from and plotted rebellion with. The organisations and campaigns I'm part of or have been a part of, and the many comrades who lent me books, recommended me films, were patient with my political journey, and who showed me the beauty of dignity, respect and compassion.

For my second family at number three – Zak, Kennedy, Maddy and Alex. Our conversations, meals, birthdays, unfinished ideas, disagreements, banners and placards, infestations and leaks, late-night sessions and early morning bathroom queues, our songwriting and performances, holidays and day trips, have all provided a place of solace, a place of learning, a place of love and a place of friendship. This book owes much to your collective sharpness of mind and unwavering commitment to truth and justice, but also your encouragement and kindness.

For the #Merky Books team: Lemara Lindsay-Prince for guiding the project, Anna Hervé for the copy-edit magic. Special thanks is owed to Tom Avery, firstly for believing in my voice and secondly for helping it find a home. Jessica Woollard, for your firm belief in my potential.

For those whose eyes over this project pushed, pulled and transformed it. Luke de Noronha for spending long evenings on the phone helping me see sense in moments of despair, and carefully guiding the early and later drafts, you're a top G. Maddy Evans for being an incredible writer to be around and on hand, a constant source of kicking up the backside and an honest critic. Rowan Kinchin for the continual support and friendship, and for really pushing me to think harder about disability, solidarity and accessibility. Tumu Johnson and Delores Baker for sharing wisdom, encouraging further enquiry and being generally badass activists. Ken Fero for your visual and educational contribution to movement building and chipping in to the resources. Adam Elliot-Cooper for doubling down on the book on more than one occasion. Natasha Mumbi Nkonde, Geneva Virasami, Alexandra Kelbert, Jonas Liston, Ramez Gadelrab, Almaz Messenger, Sivamohan Valluvan, Jay Bernard, Alison Carney and Gargi Bhattacharyya – your incisive critiques, suggestions and recommendations demonstrate both your brilliance and your generosity. Ahilapalapa Rands and Ella Grace Newton, for providing space to reflect and write, far from the British isles, for the power you bring to the struggle, and for the abundance of moments to just unwind and decompress.

For my OG's: Reece Thompson, J. P. O'Brien, Gurps, Kish, all the bruddas I grew up with. I wouldn't know the value of solidarity, of loyalty, of standing up for myself, of creativity, had it not been for the ups and downs of our shared youth. For Venus Cumara, witch and comrade, who helped mould my vision toward one led by the heart.

Finally, for Alex – this book simply wouldn't be if it weren't for you. In you I find everything I need to keep me believing, to keep me resourced and to keep me smiling. As an educator, comrade and friend, you constantly remind me of the better nature we all strive for. I'm greatly indebted to you for the time and work you've put into this book, and into me.

endNotes

INTRODUCTION

1 Ambalavener Sivanandan, *Catching History on the Wing* (London: Pluto Press, 2008), p. 11.

EDUCATE

1 Beverley Bryan, Stella Dadzie and Suzanne Scafe, *Heart of the Race: Black Women's Lives in Britain* (London: Virago, 1985), p. 58.

2 https://neu.org.uk/child-poverty-facts

3 Noam Chomsky, 'Force and Opinion', *Z Magazine*, July–August 1991.

4 bell hooks, *Feminism is for Everybody* (London: Pluto Press, 2000), p. 199.

5 Steve Biko, *I Write What I Like* (London: Bowerdean Press, 1978), p. 68.

6 James Baldwin, 'Stranger In The Village', *Notes of a Native Son* (Boston: Beacon Press, 1955), p. 119.

7   Stuart Hall, 'Old and New Identities, Old and New Ethnicities', in Anthony King, *Culture, Globalization and the World System* (Minnesota: University of Minnesota Press, 1991), p. 48.

8   Howard Zinn, *People's History of the United States* (New York: HarperCollins, 2003), p. 414.

9   A. Sivanandan, 'Catching History on the Wing: conference speech', Race & Class 50, 2009, p. 94.

10 Robin D.G. Kelley, *Freedom Dream: The Black Radical Imagination* (Boston: Beacon Press, 2002), p. 12.

11 Malcolm X, *The Autobiography of Malcolm X* (New York: Ballantine Books; Reissue Edition, 1992), p. 182.

ORGANISE

1   Paolo Freire, *Pedagogy of the Oppressed*, trans. Myra Bergman Ramos (London: Sheed and Ward, 1979), p. 34.

2   Robin D. G. Kelley, *Hammer and Hoe: Alabama Communists during the Great Depression* (North Carolina: University of North Carolina, 2015).

3 Marshall Ganz, *Why David Sometimes Wins* (Oxford University Press, USA; Reprint Edition, 2010), p. 8.

4 https://janemcalevey.com/wp-content/uploads/2013/08/new_labor_forum_takes_a_community.pdf

5 https://americanstudies.yale.edu/sites/default/files/files/Keyword%20Coalition_Readings.pdf

6 Thich Nhất Hạnh, 'Dharma Talk', *Finding Our True Heritage*, 1993.

7 Angela Y Davis, *Are Prisons Obsolete?* (North Carolina: Seven Stories Press, 2003), p. 16.

8 Mariame Kaba and Shira Hassan, *Fumbling Towards Repair: A Workbook for Community Accountability Facilitators* (California: Project NIA/Just Practice, 2019).

9 House of Commons, The UN Inquiry into the Rights of Persons with Disabilities in the UK (https://commonslibrary.parliament.uk/research-briefings/cbp-7367/).

10 Audre Lorde, 'The Master's Tools Will Never Dismantle the Master's House', *Sister Outsider: Essays and Speeches* (Crossing Press, 1984).

11 Mia Mingus, 'Changing the Framework', Leaving Evidence, 2011.

12 Leah Lakshmi, *Care Work: Dreaming Disability Justice* (Vancouver: Arsenal Pulp Press, 2018), p. 65.

13 *Activists and the Surveillance State: Learning from Repression*, ed. Aziz Choudry (London: Pluto Books, 2019), p. 13. *Activists and the Surveillance State* is an important analysis of the surveillance state, its origins and its impacts, from the perspective of those who have been subjected to its repression. D'Souza's chapter, 'The Surveillance State', is a great primer in understanding how the all-watching, all-controlling surveillance state came to into being and how it shapes global society.

14 https://www.versobooks.com/blogs/4759-the-imperial-boomerang-or-why-the-left-needs-anti-imperialism

15 https://www.jacobinmag.com/2018/04/uk-infiltration-secret-police-mi5-special-branch-undercover

16 Shiv Malik, writing for the *Guardian*, 'Occupy London's anger over police "terrorism" document', 2011.

17 https://bigbrotherwatch.org.uk/campaigns/
   stop-facial-recognition/

AGITATE

1 *Fighting for Ourselves: Anarcho-syndicalism and the Class Struggle* (London: Solidarity Federation and Freedom Press, 2012).

2 Markus Rediker, 'A Motley Crew for Our Times?', Radical Philosophy, Spring 2020.

3 An Xiao Mina, *Memes to Movements: How the World's Most Viral Media is Changing Soicial Protest and Power* (Boston: Beacon Press, 2019).

4 Akinyele Omowale Umoja, *We Will Shoot Back: Armed Resistance in the Mississippi Freedom Movement* (New York: New York University Press, 2013), p. 3.

5 Ta-Nehisi Coates, 'Barack Obama, Ferguson, and the Evidence of Things Unsaid', *The Atlantic*, 26 November 2014.

6 Nicholas Wroe, 'I did my own thing', *Guardian*, 8 March 2008.

7 Amilcar Cabral, trans. Richard Handyside, *Revolution in Guinea* (New York: Monthly Review Press, 1974), pp. 126–132.

8 Beverley Bryan, Stella Dadzie and Suzanne Scafe, *Heart of the Race: Black Women's Lives in Britain* (London: Virago, 1985), p. 138.

9 Zillah R. Eisenstein (ed.), *Capitalist Patriarchy and the Case for Socialist Feminism* (New York: Monthly Review Press), p. 362.

10 https://americanstudies.yale.edu/sites/default/files/files/Keyword%20Coalition_Readings.pdf

everyday resources

Now that you're up to speed with key lessons and the history of activism, here are a few initial steps to consider in order get right into it.

1. JOIN A UNION!

The fight against corporate companies and private landlords is the fight of our lives. Becoming a trade unionist, building the power of organised labour is crucial, so head over to the Trade Union Congress website and find your union. Getting involved with radical, grassroots unions is especially important, so make sure to check out, support or join groups like United Voices of the World (UVW), Independent Workers' Union of Great Britain (IWGB) and the London Renters' Union (LRU).

2. JOIN AN ORGANISATION!

There are thousands of important campaigns, grassroots groups and national movements out there. I've had the honour of fighting with or alongside many of them. If you search hard enough,

243

send messages, ask questions, both on the internet and in community centres, you'll find a good place to get started with activism. If the group doesn't work for you, or doesn't exist, then find people in your area and set up your own organisation and get organising, using tips from this book and elsewhere. Below are a small handful of organisations.

CLIMATE JUSTICE:
Wretched of the Earth, Green Anti-Capitalist Front, War on Want, Platform London.

DISABILITY JUSTICE:
Disabled People against Cuts, Sisters of Frida, Greater Manchester Coalition of Disabled People.

FEMINISM:
Women's Strike, Sisters Uncut.

IMMIGRATION:
Unity Centre, SOAS Detainee Support, Anti Raids Network, Detention Action, Migrants Organise, Manchester Migrant Solidarity, African Rainbow Family.

Northern Police Monitoring Project, 4Front, London Campaign against Police and State Violence, Black Lives Matter UK, Joint Enterprise Not Guilty by Association, United Families and Friends Campaign, Communities Against Prison Expansion, Empty Cages Collective, Bent Bars Collective.

3. VISIT AN ARCHIVE!

Going to the archive is a great way to keep yourself educated on how political struggle is waged, and won. Here are a few archives – physical and digital for you to engage in, it's worth visiting more than once:

> *The Black Cultural Archives, Black Feminist Bookshop, British Library Sisterhood and after collection, East End Women's Museum in London, Feminist Archive in Leeds, George Padmore Institute, Marx Memorial Library, May Day Rooms, People's History Museum in Manchester, Rukus! Glasgow, The Tandana Archive, and the Women's Library*

4. WATCH THESE FILMS!

Film has an incredibly potent way of connecting us with the experiences of others, and the possibilities of change. Below are a handful of documentaries and films that have nurtured me and my friends.

ON IMPERIALISM

John Pilger, *The War You Don't See* (2010)

Robin Shuffield, *Thomas Sankara: The Upright Man* (2006)

Goran Olssen, *Concerning Violence* (2014)

Sufyan Omeish and Abdallah Omeish, *Occupation 101* (2006)

Jason Oser, *Let the Fire Burn* (2013)

ON WORKERS STRUGGLES

Rene Lichtman, Peter Gessner and Stewart Bird, *Finally Got the News* (1970)

Felipe Bustos Sierra, *Nae Pasaran* (2018)

Matthew Warchus, *Pride!* (2014)

ON THE BLACK BRITISH STRUGGLE

Menelik Shabazz, *Blood Ah Go Run* (1982)

Franco Rosso, *The Mangrove Nine* (1973)

Ken Fero, *Injustice* (2001)

AUTOBIOGRAPHICAL FILMS AND DOCUMENTARIES

Spike Lee, *Malcolm X* (1992)

Margarethe von Trotta, *Rosa Luxemburg* (1986)

Dersim Zêrevan, *Sara* (2016)

Patty Berne, *Sin Invalid: An Unashamed Claim to Beauty* (2013)

James Lebrecht, Nicole Newnham, *Crip Camp: A Disability Revolution* (2020)

David France, *How to survive a plague* (2013)

5. READ THESE BOOKS!

First off, get yourself over to a radical bookstore, of which we have a long proud tradition across the country. Whether it's Housmans Bookshop or New Beacon in London. News from Nowhere in Liverpool, or Calton Books in Glasgow, I highly recommend you search online for your closest store and get to know it.

Below is a small sample of some books that myself and friends found as great places for continued learning. I highly recommend heading over to the extended online Everyday Resources to choose from a bigger selection. Don't forget there's a few references throughout the text which make for good additional reading.

NON-FICTION

Assata Shakur, *Assata* (Zed Books, 2014)

Audre Lorde, Zami (Crossing Press, 2001)

Malcolm X and Alex Haley, *Autobiography of Malcolm X* (Penguin Classics, 2001)

Carole Boyce Davies, *Left of Karl Marx* (Duke University Press, 2008)

Dennis Banks, Ojibwa Warrior (University of Oklahoma Press, 2005)

Work, money and economics are often overlooked. These are a good start:

Ha-Joon Chang, *Bad Samaritans* (Bloomsbury Press, 2007)

Ben Tippet, *Split: Class Divides Uncovered* (Pluto, 2020)

Naomi Klein, *No Logo* (Flamingo, 2000)

ON RACE, CLASS, COLONIALISM AND EMPIRE

Walter Rodney, *How Europe Underdeveloped Africa* (Pambazuka Press, 2012)

Beverley Bryan, Stella Dadzie and Suzanne Scafe, *The Heart of the Race* (Verso, 2018)

Peter Fryer, *Staying Power* (Pluto Press, 2018)

Kwame Ture, *Black Power* (Vintage Books, 1992)

Howard Zinn, *A People's History of the United States* (Harper Perennial, 2005)

Patrick Wolfe, *Traces of History* (Verso Books, 2015)

Patrisse Khan Cullors and Asha Bandele, *When They Call You a Terrorist* (Wednesday Books, 2020)

ON FEMINISM (AND OFTEN MUCH MORE)

Lola Olufemi, *Feminism, Interrupted* (Pluto Press, 2020)

Cinzia Arruzza, Nancy Fraser, and Tithi Bhattacharya, *Feminism for the 99%* (Verso, 2019)

bell hooks, *Feminism is for Everybody* (Pluto Press, 2000)

S. Grewal, Jackie Kay, Liliane Landor, Gail Lewis and Pratibha Parmar, *Charting The Journey* (Sheba Feminist Press, 1988)

My spiritual grounding and commitment to love as a force for change comes from watching, listening to and reading the literature of Thích Nhất Hạnh, Amma, Hazrat Inayat Khan, Thomas Merton and many more. Thích Nhất Hạnh in particular has helped me cultivate the mindfulness and appreciation of interbeing, in turn making life softer and more joyful.

FICTION

Adrienne Maree Brown and Walidah Imarisha, *Octavia's Brood* (AK Press, 2015)

Leslie Feinberg, *Stone Butch Blues* (Firebrand, 1993)

Toni Morrison, *Beloved* (Everyman, 2006)

Arundhati Roy, *God of Small Things* (HarperCollins, 1998)

James Baldwin, *Go Tell it on the Mountain* (Penguin, 2001)

Octavia E. Butler, *Parable of the Sower* (Four Walls Eight Windows, 1993)

Marge Piercy, *Woman on the Edge of Time* (Random House USA, 1998)

Gabriel Garcia Marquez, *Love in the Time of Cholera* (Vintage International, 2003)

POETRY

Jay Bernard, Hadiru Mahdi, Stacy Ann Chinn, June Jordan, Kae Tempest, Hafez, Shareefa Energy, Warsan Shire, Anthony Anaxagorou, Caleb Femi, Saul Williams, Potent Whisper, Amir Suleiman, Audre Lorde, Ben Okri, Nayyirah Waheed, Travis Alabanza. I also want to a big shout out to three visual artists who continue to inspire and educate me: Jacob V Joyce, Rudy Loewe and Tamara-Jade Kaz.

6. START A LEARNING GROUP!

Start your own *How To Change It* learning group, where you can read, watch and talk about anything from the above, get to know each other, and see where you go from there.

NOTES

NOTES

NOTES

NOTES

NOTES

NOTES

NOTES